MY FATHER'S KAMPUNG
A HISTORY OF AUKANG AND PUNGGOL

Published by
World Scientific Publishing Co. Pte. Ltd.
5 Toh Tuck Link, Singapore 596224
USA office: 27 Warren Street, Suite 401-402, Hackensack, NJ 07601
UK office: 57 Shelton Street, Covent Garden, London WC2H 9HE

Library of Congress Cataloging-in-Publication Data
Names: Seah, Shawn.
　Title: My father's kampung : a history of Aukang and Punggol / Shawn Seah.
Description: Singapore : World Scientific Publishing Co Pte Ltd, [2020] |
　Includes bibliographical references.
Identifiers: OCN 1183355676 | 978-981-122-690-8 (paperback) |
　ISBN 978-981-122-668-7 (hardcover)
Subjects: LCSH: Hougang (Singapore)--History. | Punggol (Singapore)-- History. |
　Hougang (Singapore)--Social life and customs. | Punggol (Singapore)--Social life and customs.
Classification: DDC 959.57--dc23

British Library Cataloguing-in-Publication Data
A catalogue record for this book is available from the British Library.

Copyright © 2021 by World Scientific Publishing Co. Pte. Ltd.

All rights reserved. This book, or parts thereof, may not be reproduced in any form or by any means, electronic or mechanical, including photocopying, recording or any information storage and retrieval system now known or to be invented, without written permission from the publisher.

For photocopying of material in this volume, please pay a copying fee through the Copyright Clearance Center, Inc., 222 Rosewood Drive, Danvers, MA 01923, USA. In this case permission to photocopy is not required from the publisher.

Desk Editor: Sylvia Koh

The views expressed here in this book are solely those of the author in his private capacity and do not in any way represent the views of the National Heritage Board and/or any government agencies.

Supported by

MY FATHER'S KAMPUNG
A HISTORY OF AUKANG AND PUNGGOL

SHAWN SEAH

Endorsement for
My Father's Kampung

Shawn's book takes us on a wonderful journey that explores a part of Singapore that no longer exists on local maps. Through meticulous research in the archives and interviews, he has put together a book that tells the history of Aukang. But this is not simply a "History of..." book. This book weaves together a story of one man's search for his family's past, the stories he discovered, and the history of Aukang and Hougang, and its Catholic community. It presents the history of a place through the personal stories and memories of those who once lived there. His book ensures that local memories of a place and community live on.

Dr John Kwok,
Research Fellow

The Montfort Alumni is proud to support this book by Shawn Seah which documents in great detail the history of Aukang, incorporating the long and distinguished history of Montfort School.

Montfort Alumni

Colourful, cultural, and creative: Shawn Seah's book is an excellent read. It is not easy to make history accessible but this dynamic young man has managed to bring local history alive. We strongly support his efforts in the area of writing about local culture and heritage.

Jeremy Seah,
Executive Committee Member, Singapore Seah Clan Association

I've always had a special place in my heart for Hougang's history and the culture of the Teochew Catholics. Shawn Seah's book is not to be missed, for all Aukang-nang, as well as those interested in the history of this unique enclave.

Bryan Goh,
Hougang Resident

Shawn: this is a man who is deeply passionate about his heritage.

Victor Yue,
Heritage Enthusiast

Reading this work is like unveiling a time capsule for the area we now know as Hougang. Skilfully drawing on historical developments and relevant personal anecdotes, Shawn breathes life and colour into the Aukang of yesteryear. His effort serves well to educate the next generation of Singaporeans that underpinning our modern metropolis is a rich history which should be remembered.

Joseph Tan,
Former Educator and Republic of Singapore Air Force Pilot

Shawn Seah is a true inspiration in his efforts to promote and preserve local history and identity. He absolutely dazzles with his passion and talent.

Dr Kenneth Lay,
Researcher

In recent years, there has been a growing interest in documenting Singapore's yesteryears. This yearning for the past is unsurprising as Singaporeans find themselves grappling with issues of memory and identity. However, the past offers much more than just nostalgia. It gives us learning lessons and anchors us to an identity beyond our personal history.

In my Master's thesis, I recognised the current state of urban renewal and the ever-evolving identity of communities. Using Aukang, one of Singapore's most urbanised areas with an intriguing history, as the site of intervention, my project sought to create a paradigm that other neighbourhoods could take on. Aukang-Nang (Aukang People) identify themselves with a common language— and religion— Teochew and Catholicism, respectively. The beauty of Aukang is that it embraces people of all religions and ethnicities, and harmonises Western beliefs with Chinese culture, all within a trinitarian rhythm of parish, school, and neighbourhood. However, even with its displaced community and urbanscape, the "Aukang spirit" still lives on socially and culturally through rituals and story-telling.

I am so happy to see someone like Shawn Seah, with the same interest, being so proactive about it. I support his efforts to promote local history and heritage.

Sean Yeo Ze Wei,
Teochew Singaporean

Foreword
By Robert Yeo
Poet, playwright, and author of
Routes 1940-75: A Singaporean Memoir

I lived in Valley Road, Singapore, for 26 years. From 1940 to September 1966, when I left for London for further studies, it was the only home I knew, the house of my father and his father. I walked to Serangoon English School on Simon Road and played on Valley Road, so called because the road inclined a little downhill, enough to present a problem to hawkers on bicycles. There was a famous bakery there owned by a Hainanese family. Head up Upper Serangoon Road and to the right was Lim Ah Pin Road, home to the community centre and Boys' Club where I played table tennis.

I could go on writing about my kampung, but I will not have to, as now I have found a book that does it for me, better than I could.

I am delighted to contribute this foreword for the following reasons. First, Shawn Seah reminds me of people and places I know of, and second, of people and places I did not know of. That he is able to do so is a tribute to his passion and scholarship in documenting the social history of Hougang, or Aukang as it was then called before the HDB came in.

He has wisely chosen to see a large part of it through the eyes of his father and thus has performed a wonderful filial duty. Additionally, he has personalised his narrative so that it is not a dry, objective account but a highly-individualised one. The lively interviews with prominent Teochews of the area and the apt photos and illustrations all add up to a comprehensive and intriguing tale.

A third reason for recommending this book is that, while he focuses on the Teochew Catholics, he has included those who are Eurasians, Malays, Indians, Hokkien Peranakans, and others who made up the multi-ethnic composition of Aukang. The constituency is thus seen as a typical patchwork of the larger Singapore identity.

Finally, he has cleverly linked the old Aukang, which comprised the fifth and sixth mile precincts, and Kangkar and Punggol, to the new, enormous developments that is now Sengkang and other districts. In this way, he has provided continuous engagement between the OLD that his father knew with the transformed, beyond recognition—NEW.

Foreword
By Toh Tong Dee
President of Montfort Alumni

Montfort School was founded as a parish school known as Holy Innocents' English School in 1916 within the grounds of the Church of the Nativity of the Blessed Virgin Mary at Upper Serangoon Road. The building where the school was first established still stands today!

Due to the rising enrolment, the Diocese requested that the Brothers of St Gabriel take over the management of Holy Innocents' English School in 1936. In memory of the Founder of the Order, St Louis Marie-Grignion de Montfort, the school was renamed Montfort School in 1959.

The premises were expanded in phases to cope with a rising student population. In 1960, His Grace Michel Olçomendy (the first Archbishop of Singapore) blessed the extension of a wing of the school's premises.

The history of Montfort School is strongly intertwined with the Church, as well as with the old Aukang. As a result, when the time came to build a new school, it was decided that it must be located in today's Hougang. Since 1992, Montfort School has been operating at their new premises at Hougang Avenue 8.

Such stories like these, and much more, are conveyed by Shawn Seah in his book. We strongly encourage you to read this book and support a local author who has published a book on Seah Eu Chin, his ancestor as well as a pioneer in Singapore's early history.

Shawn was inspired to trace his father's roots as his father spent his childhood and adult days in Aukang. He did extensive research, including interviewing his father's family and friends, and other people who lived in historical Aukang. He spent weekends and holidays working on this book—a testimony to his dedication to bring the history of this part of Singapore to life.

This is also a story about a son learning about his father's memories in Montfort School as a student (1953 to 1959) and later as an educator (from 1964 to 1973) at both Montfort Junior School and Montfort Secondary.

The Montfort Alumni hopes to engage more Montfortians and strive to pass on the rich heritage of Montfort from generation to generation. The Montfort Alumni is proud to support this book by Shawn Seah which documents the long and distinguished history of Montfort School.

I trust you will enjoy reading this book!

Simply Put, What is This Book About?

This book is about my father's kampung, when it was still known as Aukang, before it transformed into Hougang. This book is about a son's journey in appreciating the different life that his father experienced and understanding the history of the place he called home.

Covering the north-east of Singapore and the areas which would be called Hougang, Sengkang, Buangkok, and Punggol today, this book details my father's childhood experiences from the 1950s to 1970s. It describes memories of places, people, and professions; it evokes memories. It highlights especially the unique and distinct identity of the Catholic Teochews, but captures the stories of other communities who lived in the area. It also examines the little-known history of Aukang and Punggol in the 19th and early 20th centuries.

This book also consists of a series of wider reflections, on topics like the Kampung Spirit, identity, and the Singapore Story. In particular, the Singapore Story comprises many personal and community stories. Our unique past connects us with our present, like an anchor providing ballast in the waters of an uncertain world. I hope this book can serve as an invitation to start broader dialogues and conversations on such topics.

Contents

Foreword by Robert Yeo VIII
Foreword by Toh Tong Dee IX
Simply Put, What is This Book About? XI

Prologue XV

The Teochew
The Singapore Chinese
Decline of Dialects
Teochew Food

Chapter 1: Why Did I Write This Book? 1

Chapter 2: Where was Aukang? 7

"Teochew Kingdom" of Aukang
The Historical Past

Chapter 3: Catholicism in Aukang (1853–Present) 17

The Rise of Catholicism in Aukang
Montfort School (1916–Present)
The Church of the Nativity of the Blessed Virgin Mary (1853–Present)

Chapter 4: World at War (1914–1945) 39

The Japanese Cemetery Park in Aukang
Prostitutes, Spies, and Soldiers
World War II and The Punggol Zoo
Fortifications
The Punggol Massacres
A Safe Haven at Surin Lane
Japanese Opium Dealers?
Suffering Under the Japanese
Catholic Mass for the Departed Souls

Chapter 5: Memories of Gor Kor Chiok (Fifth Milestone) 55
Church of the Immaculate Heart of Mary
Tou Mu Kung Temple
St Paul's Church
Masjid Haji Yusoff
Teochew Cemetery
Lim Tua Tow Market
The Original Site of Da Qiao School at Lim Tua Tow Road

Chapter 6: Memories of Lak Kor Chiok (Sixth Milestone) 67
Memories of Simon Road
Serangoon English School and its Prominent Alumni
The Stories of Joo Hong Road, Lim Ah Pin Road, and Florence Road
The Upper Serangoon Community Centre and Boys' Club
Tua Jia Kar Village

Chapter 7: Memories of Kangkar (1900s-1986) 79
Kangkar Fishing Village
Kangkar Through the Eyes of Mr Lee Boon Kee
Kangkar Through the Eyes of Mr Ng Kok Song
Other Memories of Kangkar
The Last Kampung in Singapore—Kampong Lorong Buangkok

Chapter 8: Memories of Punggol 95
Memories of Punggol from the Eyes of Ng Yew Kang
The "Haunted House"—Punggol's Matilda House

Chapter 9: Kampung Memories (1946-1975) 103
Everyday Life: Houses
Utilities: Water, "Bath and Toilet" Facilities, Public Standpipes
Electricity, Pressure Lamps, and Private Generators
Transport
Entertainment
Crocodiles, a Bear, and a Python
Badminton Parties
Movies in the 1950s and 60s
Gambling

Fighting Fish and Other Animals
Banning Firecrackers Long Before the Government Did
Teochew Opera
Eking Out a Living
Private School
Travelling Hawkers or Street Hawkers
Commercial Farming

Epilogue 143

Bibliography 148

Acknowledgements 157

About the Author 159

About the Artist 160

Prologue

The Teochew

My father once told me that the Teochew people are highly refined. Instead of using crass terms, a Teochew answering the call of nature will describe the activity as a poetic reference to nature itself:

Huang lai, whole lai,
Keng chio ka lup
Sa si kai

The three key terms are: *huang* (wind), *whole* (rain), and *keng chio* (bananas). *Lai* means to come, *ka lup* means to drop, and *sa si* means three or four. Putting them altogether, the description reads:

When the wind and rain come,
The bananas drop
In threes and fours

Doesn't this poem express beautifully not only the call of nature but also the sequence in which it is answered?

Now, who makes a better bride, a Teochew or a non-Teochew Chinese?

A full-blooded Teochew lady will be totally convinced that a Teochew girl makes the best bride. Her belief may be encapsulated in a catchphrase: *Yu pi, yu chi.*

Translated into English, this can be interpreted as "Not only cheap, but also fresh". This phrase is normally what a fishmonger would say to entice customers to buy his fish.

However, used in the context of the desirability of marrying a Teochew girl, it means she is "good value for money", or, more literally, "not only cheap but good"—a less complimentary remark.

A Teochew bride is beautiful, loving, faithful, and cooks well. And, most important of all, her parents will not demand many wedding dinner tables from the in-laws! So, it is wise to marry a Teochew lass!

Finally, Teochews often refer to each other as *ka kee nang* (our own people). This refrain is repeated, by Teochew to Teochew, and sometimes in full:

Teochew nang, ka kee nang

I began a book on Aukang by telling you about the Teochews because my father is a *ka kee nang*, and he is proud of it.

The Singapore Chinese

The Singapore Chinese resident population has three major dialect groups—Hokkien, Teochew, and Cantonese. The Hokkien form the largest group, followed by the Teochew.

Historically, the Teochew were one of the earliest groups of Chinese to arrive in Singapore.[1] They came from eight districts in China, Ngee Ann being the ancient name for Chaozhou prefecture in Guangdong province where Teochews originated. According to the Teochew Poit Ip Huay Kuan, these districts were Teo Ann (Chaoan), Theng Hai (Chenghai), Teo Yeonh (Chaoyang), Kit Yeonh (Jieyang), Jeow Pheng (Raoping), Po' Leng (Puning), Hui Lye (Huilai), and Nam Oh (Nanao).

While some Teochews came to Singapore from Dapo (also Dabu, or Hakka district), language differences led to Dapo being separated from the Teochew region, leaving only eight districts, although after the 19th century, the Chinese government further divided the 8 districts into 11.

Nevertheless, in Singapore, Teochew organisations, such as the Ngee Ann Kongsi led by Teochew community leader Seah Eu Chin and the Teochew Poit Ip Huay Kuan, established later, were set up based on eight districts.

To express gratitude for a safe journey from Guangdong province to Southeast Asia, Teochew seafarers and merchants in Singapore set up a shrine dedicated to the deity Mazu, the Goddess of the Sea, in the 1820s.

Subsequently, another temple was established, called the Lao Ye Temple, or Lau Ya Keng, dedicated to Xuan Tian Shang Di (commonly known as Lao Ye), the ancestral deity of the Teochews.

These two temples were merged in 1826 and the resulting temple was named the Yue Hai Ching Temple. Although the temple was founded by Teochews, its patrons also included many Cantonese. The temple has been managed by the Ngee Ann Kongsi since 1845 and has undergone several rounds of expansion, renovation, and reconstruction. In 1899, the temple was bestowed with "peaceful clouds over the ocean at dawn" by Emperor Guangxu of the Qing dynasty.[2] Singapore's oldest Teochew temple was gazetted as a national monument in 1996.

Historically, many Teochews were involved in the planting of gambier and pepper in the Riau Archipelago even before the arrival of the British, and contributed greatly to the opening up of the interior of our island, beyond the Singapore River area.[3]

They were also deeply involved in the import and export business of goods and services. For example, my ancestor, Teochew merchant Seah Eu Chin (1805–1883),

Yueh Hai Ching Temple (or Wak Hai Cheng Bio) is the oldest Teochew temple in Singapore and a national monument.

bought and sold goods such as local produce and necessities to supply the junk trade between Singapore and the Riau islands, Sumatra, and other ports in the Malay Peninsula, and later went into the gambier and pepper business, just like other Teochews before him. Eventually, he came to be known widely as the King of Gambier and Pepper.

In 1848, in the article "The Chinese in Singapore" in the *Journal of the Indian Archipelago and Eastern Asia*, Seah Eu Chin estimated that the Chinese population was around 40,000, of which 19,000, or about half, were Teochews.

However, as growth in the number of Hokkien and Cantonese immigrants in the mid-19th century outpaced that of the Teochew, by the time the first systematic population census was undertaken in 1871, where the Chinese were accounted for by dialect groups, the Hokkiens had already overtaken the Teochews as the largest dialect group in Singapore.[4]

In 1990, there were around 896,000 Hokkiens and 466,000 Teochews.[5] A decade later, there were more than one million Hokkiens and 526,000 Teochews. Collectively, Hokkiens, Teochews, and Cantonese formed three-quarters of the Singapore Chinese population, and the remaining quarter consisted of at least 19 other dialect groups in Singapore.

In 2010, there were 562,000 Teochews out of 2.8 million local Chinese, making the Teochew community slightly above 20 percent of the Chinese in Singapore.[6] In comparison, the Hokkien community was around 1.1 million (40 percent) strong, the Cantonese were around 410,000 (15 percent), and all other Chinese dialect groups made up about 700,000 (25 percent).

With that many Teochews in Singapore, one would think that the Teochew dialect would be widely spoken.

However, that is not the case.

Decline of Dialects

Over the years, there has been an overall decline in the use of dialects in Singapore, not just Teochew. I am a good example of someone who cannot speak the dialect. I only know a smattering of Hokkien, which I picked up from compulsory military service.

Despite my father's best attempts to teach me how to speak Teochew, I can only utter: "thank you", "have you eaten", and "the monkey climbs the tree".

Starting with a series of measures in the late 1970s, Singapore's leaders discouraged the use of Chinese dialects, the original mother tongues of about three-quarters of its citizens, in favour of English and Mandarin.[7]

However, neither language had much to do with the majority of the people who lived in Singapore at the time. Ethnic Chinese, who then as now made up 75 percent of the population, had emigrated over the centuries from several mostly southern Chinese provinces, especially Fujian (where Hokkien is spoken) and Guangdong (home to Cantonese, Teochew, and Hakka). Only two percent spoke Mandarin.

In 1979, the government launched a "Speak Mandarin" campaign. And by 1981, television and radio were banned from broadcasting dialect shows, including popular music. That left many dialect speakers cut off from society, like a few of my father's aunts who could only speak Teochew.

However, the use of the Teochew dialect is still considered an important aspect of the Teochew identity, especially among the older generation in Singapore. Once, I was invited, by my friend Gary Yeo of the Singapore Teochew Group, to a dinner at the Chui Huay Lim Club. Established in 1845, it was an exclusive place for Teochew businessmen to network and relax.[8] Also known as the "Teochew Gentlemen's Club", Chui Huay Lim Club played a unique role in early Chinese society as an important social venue during the British colonial period.

There I met a Teochew author (let's call her TGL), and we talked about Teochew identity. She commented that, despite the government's repeated efforts to discourage Singaporeans from speaking dialects, "true Teochews" have still remembered how to speak Teochew.

I immediately felt a bit sheepish because I did not know how to speak Teochew, beyond a few simple phrases. While I had heard my father occasionally speak in dialect, I spoke English to my family practically all the time. Even my grandmother Joanna could speak English and we never conversed in Teochew; she reserved her Teochew mostly for her own children.

TGL also said that Teochews in southern China shared a similar identity to Teochews in Singapore, and—in the event of a dispute—would take the side of Singapore Teochews rather than the side of northern Chinese, who were considered different.

I believe her. In fact, as I have said before, "We Teochews in Singapore have a unique identity, and should be united".[9]

But for other Teochews in Singapore today, the Teochew identity is not always a big part of their personal identity. And I'm not just talking about millennials like myself, or the even younger Generation Z (well, those younger than millennials). This even affects those older than my generation.

Reporter Teo Cheng Wee, writing for *The Straits Times* in 2014, said that whenever he introduced himself to strangers, he would seldom mention that he is Teochew—not because he was ashamed to be Teochew, but his dialect group had never been a large part of his identity.[10] And he suspected that many Singaporeans felt the same way because of the government's effective discouragement of dialect use over the years. However, because his parents, and their parents before them, were all Teochew, he was able to understand Teochew and speak it well enough to hold a decent conversation, and he was in fact as Teochew as it got.

At the start, I mentioned some Teochew proverbs my father told me about. To some of the older generation in Singapore, these proverbs carry deep meaning or, at least, are poetic.

Speaking over coffee on a Sunday afternoon with my father's friend, Mr Lee Tong Juan (born 1937), I learnt a few more of these choice dialect proverbs and phrases. What makes this dialect lesson interesting is that Mr Lee is not a Teochew, but a Hainanese. He said, with what could only be described as glee in his eyes:

Let me give you some examples of rich and subtle Teochew sayings…

Pah kow, ai chai chu nang

means

Before you beat a dog, you must know who the owner is.

This implies that you have to know a person's background before you do something you might regret.

Juat neo kng kng, kway Siam lo
Ah ti oo boh, ah hia bor

means

The moon is passing through Siam
Younger brother has a wife, but the older brother doesn't

This saying is used to tease an elder brother for not being married yet, while his younger brother is already married.

Ho kow boh teng loh

means

Good dogs do not obstruct the way

This saying is that if one is well-trained, one would be useful, just like a well-trained dog would not get in the way of someone.

Chwee tiam tiam, uk buay chark kee kau niam

means

A sweet talker carries a sickle at the back.

This saying is used to refer to someone deceptive, so one has to watch out for this sort of person.

Gu kia um pat ho

means

Young cows do not know the tiger.

The implication is that they should fear the tiger.

Older folks often spoke these phrases, which may sound cryptic to some today, but are very meaningful.

My father was chuckling to himself the whole time Mr Lee was explaining these local Teochew proverbs to me.

Teochew Food

Beyond speaking the dialect, being Teochew could also be about the food. My online friends from Teochew Facebook groups frequently post pictures of the mouth-watering Teochew food they are eating. As I am not a foodie, it is hard for me to describe food. But Teo Cheng Wee can, and he vividly described his childhood experiences:

> I had countless meals of Teochew porridge with pickled cucumber, fermented beancurd, and salted egg—a meal combo which still frightens me today.
>
> But the upside was the festive Teochew food my grandmother used to make.
>
> I was only a few years old, but I remember she would toil for hours to make her delicious *png kueh* (rice cakes), filled with dried shrimp, mushroom, pork and peanuts, from scratch…
>
> I also had to help *dor bee*, or **sift rice grains**, whenever the Dragon Boat Festival came around.[11]

When I read those lines he wrote, I felt really hungry. And my father and many people I interviewed had a love of Teochew cuisine. They seemed really happy when they talked about Teochew food. But most importantly, reminiscing like this helps them feel in touch with their identity most keenly.

Endnotes

1. This section is adapted from Shawn Seah, *Seah Eu Chin: His Life and Times* (Singapore: Pagesetters, 2019).

2. According to a plaque by the Urban Redevelopment Authority at the Yueh Hai Ching Temple, "Yueh Hai Ching Temple".

3. Tan Gia Lim, *An Introduction to the Culture and History of the Teochews in Singapore,* (Singapore: World Scientific, 2018), p.44. She cited several examples, such as William Farquhar's report to Raffles in 1822 and colonial government records detailing a sale of a plantation land by some planters with names likely of Teochew origin. George Yeo, then-Minister for Trade and Industry, also made a speech which referred to this fact at The Teochew Experience: An Exhibition on the Teochew Community in Singapore, 3 October 2002.

4. Ibid., p.45.

5. These statistics are based on Edmond Lee Eu Fah's paper, "Profile of the Singapore Chinese Dialect Groups", which drew from data from the Population Censuses 2000 and 1990. Incidentally, the Cantonese were number three in 2000, numbering 386,000 (in 1990, there were about 324,000).

6. Department of Statistics Singapore, *Singapore Census of Population 2010 Statistical Release 1: Demographic Characteristics, Education, Language and Religion (2011).*

7. This paragraph is based on Ian Johnson, "In Singapore, Chinese Dialects Revive After Decades of Restrictions", in *The New York Times,* 26 August 2017.

8. This section is based on Chui Huay Lim Club, "Introduction". Source: http://www.chuihuaylimclub.com/introduction.html. Updated 2013. Accessed 10 April 2019.

9. Shawn Seah, as quoted in "Teochew v Teochew: From 'twin brothers' to combatants in court", in *The Sunday Times,* 10 March 2019, p. A4.

10. This section is based on Teo Cheng Wee, "Growing Teochew Roots", in *The Straits Times,* 10 November 2014.

11. Ibid.

Chapter 1
Why Did I Write This Book?

What does the Teochew identity in Singapore have to do with my father's kampung?

My father Simon Seah Seow Kee was born in 1946, at Lorong Low Koon in Aukang, in the north-east part of Singapore. He, my uncles and aunties, and their friends and neighbours grew up in the area. My father also lived at Jalan Payoh Lai, Jalan Lye Kwee, and Lorong Buangkok for about thirty years, before he moved out of Aukang in 1975.

This part of Singapore is intriguing because Teochews are not the dominant Chinese dialect group in Singapore; Hokkiens are. In the same way, Catholicism is not the dominant religion in Singapore; Buddhism and Taoism are.

Yet, Aukang used to be a Teochew-dominated area, with many Catholic Teochews.

Several reports confirm that at various points in north-eastern Singapore's history, Teochews at Aukang were either the majority of the Chinese in the area or disproportionate to their overall size in Singapore. For example, in 1986, *The Straits Times* reported that more than 90 percent of the villagers were Teochews in areas like Kangkar in historical Aukang, with the Teochew dialect the lingua franca of the area.[1]

According to the 1957 census, more than 56,000 Teochews lived in the administrative area of Serangoon district (this was a much larger area covering not only Serangoon and Punggol, but also areas like Paya Lebar and Seletar), making it the location with the largest concentration of Teochews outside the City of Singapore, where more than 140,000 Teochews resided.[2]

When the figures are compared to the size of the total Chinese population residing in the area, Serangoon had the highest proportion of Teochews in the whole of Singapore, with more than one-third of the Chinese residents Teochew.[3]

And even earlier in 1891, when the rural population was much smaller, more than 55 percent of the 900 Chinese in Div 1 (covering north-eastern Singapore, which included areas like Aukang, Kangkar, and Punggol) were Teochews.[4]

And among the Teochews in Aukang, there were many Catholics. Academic and Hougang resident Bryan Goh used a 1973 parish census and calculated that around 70 percent of the area's residents had a distinct Catholic-Teochew communal identity.[5] My father is one of these Catholic Teochews.

While the main rural church at the heart of Aukang was the Church of the Nativity of the Blessed Virgin Mary (which started as a much smaller chapel in 1853), there was also the Church of the Immaculate Heart of Mary (which started as a chapel in 1953) between the fifth and sixth milestones of Upper Serangoon, and St Anne's Church in Punggol (since 1963).

My father once told me about his heritage: "I am Teochew and proud of it. Without my Teochew heritage, I would be culturally lost as I speak no Mandarin. Besides, almost all the neighbours at that time were Teochew."

But what is even more unique is that Singapore Teochew is a localised one, different from the one in China.

I spoke to long-time resident Mr Ng Yew Kang, President of the Genealogy Society Singapore, who is Teochew. I asked him, "What do you think of the Teochew dialect in Singapore?"

He replied, "Singapore's Teochew dialect is a localised one, a little different from those spoken in Swatow and Teochew cities.

"There are words adapted from Malay such as *sarbun* (soap) and *pasar* (market). English words and Hokkien dialect are also used in the local Teochew dialect.

"What was unique about Hougang was that even non-Teochews, including Indians, could speak Teochew. I had an Indian colleague in the PA (People's Association) who could speak beautiful Teochew. In fact, poet and lecturer Professor Edwin Thumboo, whose mum was Teochew, could also speak Teochew and sing excerpts from Teochew opera."

The view that Aukang was largely populated by Teochews with a strong sense of pride in their culture and heritage was also shared by non-Teochews who lived there.

My father's Hainanese friend Tong Juan lived in Aukang for many years. He was born at North Bridge Road on 18 October 1937 to a Hainanese family from China. However, his family moved away from town when war started brewing, as his maternal grandfather said that it would be safer in the countryside. In 1941, they moved to Lorong Ah Soo. In 1942, they moved to a relative's attap house at Poh Huat Road nearby. From 1943 to 1958, his family lived at 737 Florence Road, and from 1959 to 1972, his family moved to 189P Florence Road.

One day, over tea, I asked Tong Juan, "As a Hainanese living in Aukang looking into the community, what did you think of the Teochews?"

He replied without hesitation, "In Aukang, the majority of the Teochews are friendly, approachable, and helpful. My good friends and school buddies are all Teochews. I have never been treated like a minority by the Teochews, and everyone spoke the same dialect."

He also said that he knew a lot more about the Teochew dialect and its proverbs than the Hainanese dialect. He said, "I have imbued a lot of Teochew culture, and know more Teochew proverbs than Hainanese proverbs.

"This was because all my neighbours were Teochew, and Holy Innocents' English School, where I studied, was also full of Teochews; the lingua franca at the time was Teochew, and even the teachers spoke Teochew to the students.

"Indian and Malay boys coming from Punggol to Holy Innocents' English School could all speak Teochew, including your father's neighbours Ahmad and Ali."

Tong Juan continued, "My wife and all my younger brothers' wives were Teochew. My wife can understand Hainanese but cannot speak it, but I can speak fluent Teochew."

I also spoke to a Peranakan who lived in Aukang. Over lunch at The Peranakan (of course!) at Orchard Road with local poet, writer, and playwright Baba Robert Yeo Cheng Chuan, I learnt about his childhood home.

Born 27 January 1940, Robert lived at 5 Valley Road, off Upper Serangoon Road, in a wooden bungalow house. It belonged to his paternal grandfather, Yeo Teck Hock. In Valley Road, the Yeo family was the only Hokkien Peranakan family; the Pakeri family was the only Indian family. The rest were Teochews. As Robert wrote in his memoir, *Routes:*

> **I was part of a Baba family, one of the very few, living in a predominantly Teochew community six miles from the city. But six miles from the city was a psychological distance from both a recognisable location where matters of national interest were transacted, and a major city road, which for me was Bras Basah Road. A Singapore Traction Company bus boarded just atop Valley Road would take us to the city on a relatively straight road from Upper Serangoon Road, through Serangoon Road, Selegie Road and into Bras Basah Road. Returning home from Bras Basah Road on a bus or a taxi, we would say *Owkang* [sic] or *Lak Kor* [author's note: referring to *Lak Kor Chiok* or the sixth milestone] and pay the appropriate fare.[6]**

Robert could speak a smattering of Teochew, and spoke chiefly Baba Malay and English.[7] Actually, reading *Routes* convinced me that his idea of "smattering" was a level of Teochew higher than what the younger generation can command today.

However, he once unfortunately faced a rude rebuke in Teochew from a *towkay neo* (lady boss) of a provision shop who was fierce and unsmiling, and spoke no English: *"Turng nang buay heow tar turng nang whay"*.

Having faced this comment myself a few times before, which means "A Chinese man who cannot speak Chinese", I definitely empathised with Robert. I have been at the receiving end of a similar comment in Malay: *Orang Cina Bukan Cina,* or OCBC (nothing to do with the name of the local bank)! But Robert's experience did demonstrate how strongly some people felt about Teochew culture in Aukang.

Over the years, I have discovered what the past was like from speaking with my father and relatives, and their friends, and other people who have lived in Aukang. As a result, I have come to learn more about Teochew culture and heritage. And this has been a good chance to connect with my father and uncles, as family has become increasingly important to me.

If we do not document my father's personal stories and memories of his former kampung, as well as the stories of others who lived there, we would eventually lose something intangible but valuable.

Beyond looking at the experiences of the 1940s to 1970s when my father lived in Aukang, my father and I have also examined where we can position Aukang's history. This book covers the history of Aukang and Punggol from its early days, such as its founding as a Malay kampung which preceded Singapore's founding by Raffles in 1819. It focuses mainly on the Teochew community, who dominated the Chinese in the area, and highlights the unique history and identity of the Catholic Teochews.

It also tells stories of many Teochews who came from this rural, north-eastern part of Singapore, for example, educator and poet Benedict Teo Kah Leng and pioneer poet Paul Teo Poh Leng; politicians Goh Chew Chua, Ng Kah Ting, and Lim Choon Mong; former Chief Investment Officer Ng Kok Song; former senior civil servant Ng Yew Kang; former principal Lee Boon Kee; and many others.

However, due to the limitations of space, it is unfortunately impossible to cover all the prominent Teochews who came from north-eastern Singapore. Take for example some successful businessmen from humble rural beginnings: businessman Chua Kee Teang once lived at 225 Punggol Road, in a vegetable and poultry farming family, and studied at Xinmin Secondary School from 1961 to 1964, a village school set up by Yap Fun Fong in 1945;[8] the successful founder of Leco Motor, Ng Hoy Keng, was born in a Punggol kampung in 1945, the sixth of eight siblings;[9] and Koh Yang Kee, who lived in Punggol during his childhood years and whose father was a fisherman, rose from humble beginnings, from driving container trucks for 15 years to becoming a logistics leader in 12 countries, with 1,250 employees, and around four million square feet in warehouse space.[10] No one book could do justice to the many successful Teochews and their stories.

This book also examines other groups of people who resided in the area, such as the other Chinese dialect groups, Malays, Indians, Eurasians, and Catholic missionaries like the Gabrielite Brothers. The stories of prominent non-Teochew personalities who lived in Aukang, like Robert Yeo, EW Barker, and Percival Aroozoo, are also covered in this book. And the book even covers Japanese sex workers, spies, and soldiers... well, at least, their remains in Aukang.

While it is as comprehensive as I can make it, the book will not cover everything and does not aim to do so, because north-east Singapore has such a long, complex, and rich history.

Moreover, the history of any place or community in Singapore is not a complete canvas hiding in the dark waiting for light to be shone upon it, but in a constant process of being uncovered, discovered, and rediscovered.

I hope that the history and stories which I have uncovered, discovered, and rediscovered can help to give a sketch of what my father's kampung was like before, and after, he was born.

If this book inspires more people to find out about the history of places and spaces in Singapore, and the stories of those who have come before us, all the better. And if it can provoke broader reflection, dialogue, or discussion, I would be delighted.

Endnotes

1. Augustine Low, "Kangkar, once noted for fresh fish and Teochews", in *The Straits Times*, 30 September 1986, p. 16.

2. Chua Seng Chew, *Report on the Census of Population 1957*, (Singapore: Lim Bian Han, Government Printer, Singapore, 1964), p. 146.

3. Proportions paint a more accurate picture than absolute sizes. This is because while there were more than 140,000 Teochews in the City of Singapore, there were more than 700,000 Chinese of many dialect groups residing in the area. In contrast, only about 165,000 Chinese resided in Serangoon.

4. Report on the Census of the Straits Settlements, cited in Tan Gia Lim, *An Introduction to the Culture and History of the Teochews in Singapore*, (Singapore: World Scientific, 2018), p. 50.

5. Bryan Goh, "The Catholic-Teochew Rhythm: Communal Identity in Hougang, 1945–1981", *Sojourn: Journal of Social Issues in Southeast Asia*, Vol. 33, No. 1, March 2018, p. 228.

6. Robert Yeo, *Routes: A Singaporean Memoir 1940–75* (Singapore: Ethos Books, 2014), p. 40.

7. Ibid., pp. 39–40.

8. Leong Ching, "Chua Kee Teang: Possibilities in Thorny Problems", in *The Story of Singapore Teochews* (Singapore: Teochew Poit Ip Huay Kuan, 2018), pp. 28–30.

9. Tan Kog Enn, "Ng Hoy Keng: Driving Ambition", in *The Story of Singapore Teochews* (Singapore: Teochew Poit Ip Huay Kuan, 2018), pp. 80–83.

10. Choo Woon Hock, "Koh Yang Kee: From Truck Driver to Logistics Leader", ibid., pp. 122–123.

Chapter 2
Where was Aukang?

Hougang, as we know it today, is huge. In 2018, it was Singapore's largest public housing estate based on land area, with an estimated 179,500 Housing & Development Board (HDB) residents and with HDB managing more than 54,000 flats.[1] Based on 2017 data, Hougang was more than 1,300 hectares (roughly over 1,300 football fields in size), while Woodlands was the second largest at 1,260 hectares and Tampines was the third largest at 1,200 hectares.

Some readers may think that Hougang and Aukang are the same place. When I first started on this project, I thought that way too. And in a sense the term "Aukang" is the Teochew version of "Hougang", the Romanised version of the same name in Mandarin. Aukang in Teochew means "back harbour". The opposite harbour—the one at the front—referred to Keppel Harbour in Singapore's south.[2]

So surely, my father's kampung of Aukang was just Hougang—back then. All that was needed was to trace Hougang's history.

However, my father corrected my initial view.

He said, "Geographically, these two may not be exactly the same area, since parts of Aukang then are not considered parts of Hougang now."

"Huh?" I said, confused.

"For example, Kangkar—a fishing village—was part of Aukang, but is not part of Hougang today. Parts of Kangkar are now Sengkang.

"Basically, what constitutes the actual location or area of Aukang itself can be quite controversial. It can vary according to the person you ask."

According to my father: "Aukang refers to the stretch of Upper Serangoon, from the fifth milestone intersection of Upper Paya Lebar and Upper Serangoon Road up to the seventh milestone, called Kangkar. It also includes Punggol, the whole of Punggol.

"There are also some people, like your mother, who believe that Aukang was even bigger, beginning from the third milestone, Wan Tho Avenue. But I don't necessarily hold that view. So, some think the place is bigger, while others think the place is smaller."

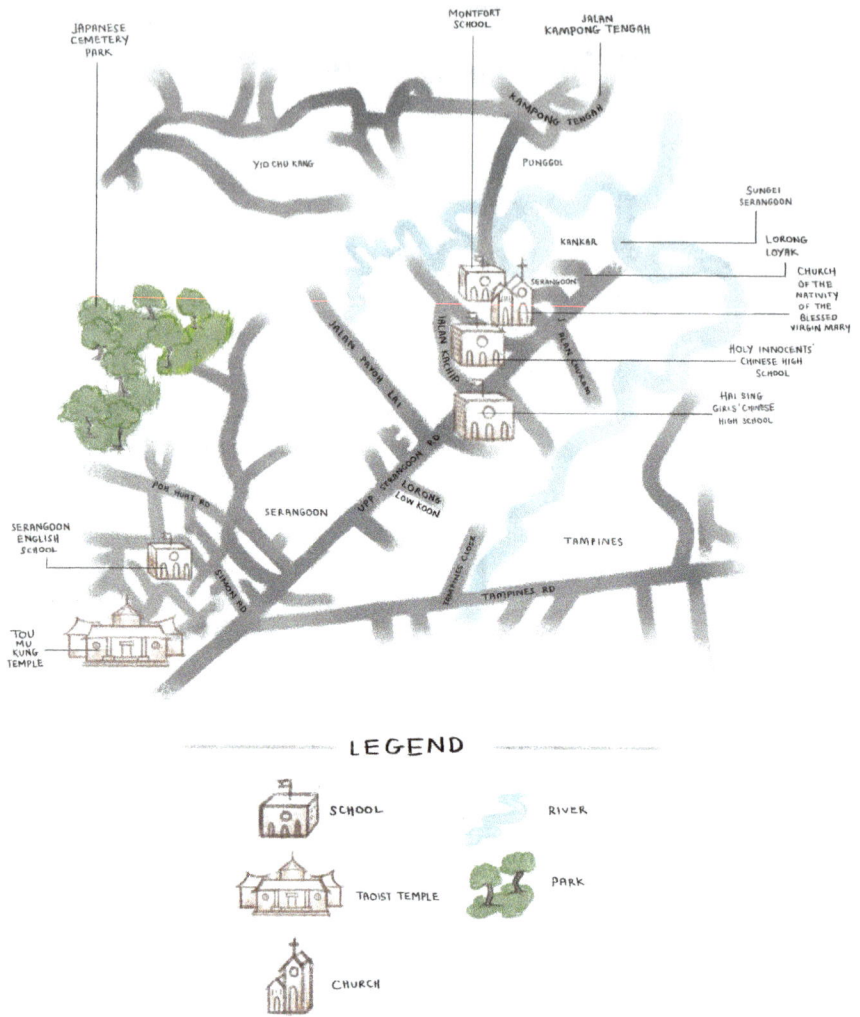

An artist's impression of historical Aukang circa 1950s.

Incidentally, milestones during my father's time—literally large stones placed at intervals from each other—were used to mark or indicate important places by how far they were relative to the General Post Office (GPO) at Fullerton Building. This is where Fullerton Hotel is located today.[3] For example, the fifth milestone was nearer to the GPO compared to the sixth milestone. Eventually, as rural villages disappeared and Singapore developed a more comprehensive address system, milestones gradually disappeared from everyday use.

Where was Aukang?

My father continued, "However, things get more complicated. In the 1950s and 1960s, the political constituency was even called Punggol, instead of Hougang. In the 1955 State Assembly elections, the electoral division called Punggol-Tampines also covered Aukang, then part of Punggol."

Incidentally, Teochew Goh Chew Chua, one of the three successful PAP candidates in the 1955 State Assembly elections—the other two being Lee Kuan Yew and Lim Chin Siong—lived in Aukang.[4] In 1955, Goh contested in the Punggol-Tampines division, which included Aukang. While more than 29,000 lived in Punggol-Tampines, only about 6,600 were electors, of which 4,500 were Chinese. Goh was later re-elected in Tampines constituency in 1959 and appointed Parliamentary Secretary to the Deputy Prime Minister. He passed away in 1971.

My father continued, "In other words, what was named Punggol constituency really referred to what are Hougang and Punggol today, so in the same speech, in one moment, the Member of Parliament could be referring to one part of Punggol—that is to say, the Hougang part—and in the very next moment, referring to Punggol proper. So, in a certain peculiar sense, even 'Punggol' sometimes really means 'Aukang'.

"In fact, in the Legislative Assembly General Election of 1959, a distant relative of ours, Tay Keng Hock, or Hock Ku (Uncle Hock in Teochew), stood as an independent candidate for the constituency of Punggol. We used to live on his huge estate at Jalan Payoh Lai. Of the four candidates, Hock Ku brought up the rear, with less than six percent of the voters finding the coconut tree—the symbol he had chosen for his election posters—appealing."

I looked it up; it's true:

Candidates	Party	Total Votes
Ng Teng Kian	PAP	4,072 (46.39%)
Tan Jin Hong	SPA	3,655 (41.64%)
Quah Heck Peck	LSP	554 (6.31%)
Tay Keng Hock	-	497 (5.66%)

Source: 1959 Legislative Assembly General Election results from the Elections Department.

These revelations prompted me to find out more. To me, the history of a place, and to a certain extent even its geography, is messy with many twists and turns. So, while the terms "Hougang" and "Aukang" did not refer to the exact same boundaries and "Punggol" sometimes meant "Aukang", it was exciting to learn more about my father's kampung.

Later, while looking for sources on geographical boundaries I could concentrate on, I found out that Aukang had even been referred to as… a "Teochew Kingdom".

"Teochew Kingdom" of Aukang

According to an article written by Bryan Goh:

> After the Speak Mandarin Campaign in 1979, the Housing & Development Board (HDB) started referring to Hougang Town by its Mandarin-based name "Hougang" instead of the original Teochew name "Aukang". However, the two names do not refer to the exact same boundaries. Present-day Hougang Town is bordered by the Kallang-Paya Lebar Expressway, Upper Paya Lebar Road, Yio Chu Kang Road and Buangkok Drive. This covers a much larger area than the historic boundaries of Aukang which Rev. Fr. Augustine Tay calls a "Teochew Kingdom". Tay [was] the first *Aukang-nang* to become the Parish Priest (2002 to 2007) of the Roman Catholic Church of the Nativity of the Blessed Virgin Mary (Nativity Church) there.
>
> This "Teochew Kingdom" of Aukang comprised of [sic] numerous kampongs [sic] located from around the 5th milestone of Serangoon Road (around Upper Serangoon Shopping Centre today) to the fishery located at the end of Serangoon Road (around Punggol Park today).[5]

I reported my findings to my father, but he knew that already.

"Told you that Aukang was a Teochew place."

The Historical Past

One of the oldest kampungs in Singapore, Kampung Punggol (that is to say, Punggol proper, rather than part of Aukang) was here even before Raffles came, according to Penghulu Awang bin Osman, a long-time Punggol resident.[6] According to him, the kampung was founded by his great-grandfather and all its residents were related.

Two-thirds of them were fishermen.

In 1985, *The Straits Times* reported that the 500 residents of Kampung Punggol were planning a grand *kenduri* (community gathering or feast) before they went their separate ways in 1986 to start a new life in high-rise Housing Board flats. The high points in Kampung Punggol's history were framed in pictures on the walls of Mr Awang's 100-year-old house. There were pictures of Mr Richard Nixon (then US Vice-President) when he visited them. There were also pictures of then-President Yusof bin Ishak and then-Prime Minister Lee Kuan Yew on other visits. Reportedly, many of these kampung folk eventually moved to flats in Hougang.

How old is Aukang, then? Since the front harbour, Keppel Harbour, was discovered in 1848, and the first dock—Dock No. 1—was built in 1859, we can safely say that Aukang was named the way it was named sometime in the mid-19th century.

The view that Aukang and Punggol were settled during that period is a common one. According to a Punggol Community Club souvenir magazine marking the CC's official opening:[7]

> In the middle of the 19th century, most of the Chinese immigrants were engaged in plantation work after they had come to Singapore. They planted crops in the river basins around the suburbs. In the early part of the 20th Century, the planting of rubber became an important economic activity. There were many rubber trees planted in the river basins of Punggol suburbs [in this instance, Punggol could refer to either Aukang, Punggol, or both]…

There is evidence that Aukang already had settlers in the 1850s—Teochew coolies who dealt in gambier and pepper, which were usually grown together.

For example, on 28 March 1855, C. R. Rigg, Collector of Assessment and Taxes, reported to Thomas Church for his information that Mr Marquard visited 155 Plantations.[8] One of the districts was "How Kang".

And on 15 May 1855, a survey in *The Straits Times* revealed that there were 243 coolies in "How Kang", along with 27 clearings, 487,000 mature gambier trees and 120,000 young trees, 79,900 mature pepper vines and 35,700 young ones.[9]

Philip Marquard, who was in charge of Siglap Station at "Seglap District", writing on 17 October 1856 to the Deputy Superintendent in charge of the Police to report about the poor location of his police station, revealed that the "jungle inhabitants of the Howkang [sic] and Lowe Chu-Kang Baru Districts convey their produce to Town by the Serangoon Road".[10]

Back then, Aukang was a lawless place. In fact, my father once told me that an old Teochew saying went, "*Lao Aukang, bo cheng hu*"—which translated into English means, "Old Aukang is a lawless place" (literally: a place with no government)!

No one would say the same about Hougang today (or Sengkang, or Buangkok, or Punggol, for that matter).

Newspaper reports before 1860 clearly show that Aukang was a lawless area just as my father had suspected. There were murders, robberies, gambling problems, secret societies, kidnappings, tiger attacks, riots (anti-Catholic riots and interracial riots), and massacres (at Punggol Road). For example, on 9 July 1850, *The Straits Times* reported:

> MURDERS—In the afternoon of the 23rd Ultimo as two Malays were proceeding in their boat with three passengers (two Klings and one Chinese) from Poogal [sic] to Serangoon they were met near the entrance of the Serangoon River by 14 Malays and a large sampan, who asked them for Tobacco; they replied they had none, when 13 of the Malays, 2 or 3 being armed with spears, jumped out of their boat into the water (which was about three feet deep) went to the other boat, and demanded their clothes, &c [sic]. One of the Malays, a Kling and the Chinese immediately jumped into the water and made for the shore, but were overtaken and stripped entirely naked with the exception of the Chinese, whose trowsers they took off and also his jacket; the other Malay and Kling were stripped near the boat and speared: the Malays then took all the articles that were in the boat, consisting of a little Rice and a few old Parangs and Chunkuls and went off towards Pulo Obin [sic].[11]

And in 1851, *The Straits Times* reported:

> On Wednesday morning last Eyo ah Toh, a gambier and pepper planter, residing at Passier Ries [sic], left that place in a boat with a quantity of pepper for sirangoon [sic] where a cart was to be in waiting to convey the pepper to town; he was accompanied in the boat by Eyo Long Soon, his cooly, and Eyo Teng You, a son of the

> owner of the boat: they reached Serangoon about 9 o'clock the same morning, and there Eyo Ah Toh met, as expected, his partner Eyo Ah Tung, with the cart; the pepper was removed from the boat to the Cart, and two bags of rice (above two piculs) were put in the boat as also four dollars in silver brought from town by Eyo Ah Tung. Eyo Long Soon and Eyo Teng You then started for Passier Ries, but not reaching that place by the afternoon their friends became alarmed, and made a search for the boat, but in vain… the following evening the boat was discovered drawn up and empty on the beach up a small creek between Serangoon and Passier Ries [sic], and near it was found the body of Eyo Long Soo, covered with what appeared to be kris wounds; the other body was found close by also wounded."[12]

1851 was a tumultuous year. It was also the year that the infamous anti-Catholic riots occurred, mainly at Kranji and Bukit Timah, but Aukang was not spared. After all, it was settled by Teochews working on the gambier and pepper plantations in the interior of Singapore, and there were Catholics among them.

Grim news:

> The interior of our Island is in fire and flame. The disturbances, robberies and burglaries have never before reached such a height…
>
> In the present case, there appears to exist a determination on the part of the heathen and secret societies to expel the christians from all the rural districts of our island. Everywhere, at Serangoon, Bukit Timah, Bookoh Khan, Lauw Choo-khan, Nam To-kang, Chan Chwee-kang, even at Kranjee, Propo and Benot the bangsals and plantations of the christians have been attacked by sets of 20 to 50 heathen, who rob all the property and destroy what they cannot carry away. The christians come to town from all parts of the country as to a place of refuge, and people yesterday in flourishing circumstances are to day reduced to the greatest misery. Not less than twenty seven plantations have been attacked and the list of planters ruined by these vagabonds on the same day…
>
> —*Free Press, February 21.*[13]

Another attack took place at the mouth of the Serangoon River in 1855. Shopkeeper Tan Joo Hok, who lived near the New Market in New Bridge Road, fortunately survived the attack.[14] As Tocksing's Pauper Hospital (today's Tan Tock Seng Hospital) stated:

> We regret to notice the frequency of murderous attacks made by small parties of Malays on the Chinese in the interior, or coming from Johor, under circumstances which scarcely warrant the supposition that plunder is the object of the attack. On the 26th [of] April no less than four wounded men were conveyed to the Hospital, who had been attacked between Changee [sic] and the Johore river. On the 16th an unarmed Chinese and his two companions, coming from Johore, were set upon by Malays. We subjoin the deposition of one of the unfortunate men who was dangerously wounded; the wound laid the chest quite bare, as broad as the palm of the hand, and another on the side from which the breath escaped at each respiration, yet strange to say the man bore his suffering in the best humour, and is in a fair way of recovering, although after being wounded he remained in the water the whole night.
>
> TOCKSING'S PAUPER HOSPITAL
April 17th, 1855 10 min. to 1 P.M.

Aukang in the 19th century, just like many parts of rural Singapore, was a dangerous and uncertain place then.

Endnotes

1 Housing & Development Board, "Hougang". Source: http://www.hdb.gov.sg/cs/infoweb/about-us/history/hdb-towns-your-home/hougang. Updated 4 October 2017. Accessed 15 August 2019.

2 According to the Marina at Keppel Bay website, Captain Henry Keppel discovered a sheltered, deep water harbour in 1848. It was known as New Harbour until April 1900, when Keppel, then the Admiral, visited Singapore again. To honour him, the Acting Governor, Sir Alexander Swettenham, renamed the harbour Keppel. The development of the harbour in mid-19th century in Singapore led to the prosperity of the island.

3 James Tann posed an interesting riddle on Facebook on 8 September 2019. The GPO was built in 1929. Where was Mile Zero, where the milestones were measured from, before the GPO was built? According to him, before 1929, milestones were measured from the Main Gate of the Balai Police Bahru, or the New Police Station, located on North Bridge Road, opposite St Andrew's Cathedral, where Capitol Piazza stands today.

4 This section is based on Pang Cheng Lian, "Lee pays respect to PAP stalwart", in *New Nation*, 29 June 1971, p. 2 and The Singapore Free Press, "The Big Vote Trek", in *The Singapore Free Press*, 19 March 1955, p. 7.

5 Bryan Goh, "Hougang: Diversity in a Teochew Enclave", in *Muse SG*, No. 38, Vol. 11, Issue 02, p. 6.

6 This section is based on Gillian Pow Chong, "A feast before the farewell", in *The Straits Times*, 12 November 1985, p. 13.

7 This section is based on Punggol Community Club, *Punggol Community Club (Official Opening) Souvenir Magazine*, 13 March 1993, Singapore, p. 9.

8 This was reported in Singapore Free Press and Mercantile Advertiser, "The Free Press", in *Singapore Free Press and Mercantile Advertiser*, 12 April 1855, p. 2.

9 These statistics are from a survey. The Straits Times, "Untitled", in *The Straits Times*, 15 May 1855, p. 5.

10 Singapore Free Press and Mercantile Advertiser, "Municipal Committee", in *Singapore Free Press and Mercantile Advertiser*, 13 November 1856, p. 3.

11 The Straits Times, "Untitled", in *The Straits Times*, 9 July 1850, p. 5.

12 The Straits Times, "Untitled", in *The Straits Times*, 28 January 1851, p. 5.

13 As reported in The Singapore Free Press and Mercantile Advertiser, "Untitled", in *The Singapore Free Press and Mercantile Advertiser*, 5 March 1851, p. 1.

14 The Straits Times, "Untitled", in *The Straits Times*, 1 May 1855, p. 4.

Chapter 3
Catholicism in Aukang (1853–Present)

The Rise of Catholicism in Aukang

One key defining characteristic of Teochew Aukang was how steeped it was in Roman Catholicism, even early on.

There has been interest in the history of Catholics in Singapore. For example, historian Dr Marc Rerceretnam conducted research on Christianised Peranakan communities in early Singapore (1830s to 1860s), with an emphasis on the Catholic church.[1]

There has also been interest in Catholic Teochews, as there were many Teochews among early converts. According to Cyprian Lim's book, *My Maternal Roots*, an important Catholic Teochew community fled from Swatow to Singapore in 1927 and 1928 to escape persecution and political unrest after the establishment of the Chinese Communist Party in 1921.[2]

Why were there so many Catholic Teochews in Aukang?

During one of our discussions, I asked my father this question, adding: "This question is quite crucial and central to the whole book."

My father had a ready answer, "This was because of the large role the Catholic missionaries played in the education of children in Aukang and the Christian schooling they brought to Singapore."

While this was an interesting view, as my father and his parents were Catholics, and he was a Montfort boy, I thought that this was just a personal view. I soon discovered some academic evidence to support my father's personal view. Bryan Goh argued in "The Catholic-Teochew Rhythm: Communal Identity in Hougang, 1945–1981":

> Three factors accounted for the distinctiveness of this community. First, the Teochew migrants arrived in Hougang before the foundation of a church there. They constituted an essentially Teochew community before the burgeoning influences of institutional Catholicism in the area. Missionaries of the Société des Missions étrangères de Paris

(MEP) had begun to convert Teochews in Shantou and its hinterlands as early as the eighteenth century… and the Catholics who began to arrive in Hougang in the early nineteenth century had their origins in that population. Only in 1857 [sic] did MEP priest Fr Ambroise Maistre purchase forty acres of land from the British East India Company to build an attap church ministering to a handful of Teochew farmers and fishermen in the area… After the establishment of the church, contacts between the MEP bishop in Shantou and the order's missionaries in Singapore resulted in a steady influx of both Catholic and non-Catholic Teochew migrants to Hougang. The physical expansion of the church to become the Neo-Gothic structure renamed the "Church of the Nativity of the Blessed Virgin Mary" in 1901 reflected the scale of that influx. The process of negotiating and amalgamating the Teochew and Catholic traditions allowed for a certain distancing from the roots of both traditions that sets the scene for the emergence of a new identity, one forged in Singapore. Second, the daily routines and ceremonial practices of about five hundred extended Teochew Catholic families congregated in close proximity on church land reinforced this communal identity. Third and last, the mission's ownership of land also allowed for an unprecedented concentration of four schools in what was still a rural setting. These schools represented the only education option in the vicinity, and their common routinised Catholic practices further fostered and enforced the Catholic-Teochew rhythm.[3]

Simply put, Catholic Teochews arrived in Aukang in its early days, around mid-1800; a church was formed to serve their needs—the Church of the Nativity—and several schools were founded by the Church; and there arose a virtuous cycle of Catholic Teochew practices and behaviours. Even foreign missionaries in Aukang could speak Teochew, or learnt it in Romanised form to communicate with the locals of Aukang.[4]

Attracted by the Teochew population at Aukang and Punggol area, and assured by their Teochew and Catholic practices, Catholic Teochew migrants from China periodically came to the area and some subsequently settled down. For example, on 27 March 1928, the *Malaya Tribune* dramatically proclaimed that Catholic refugees from Swatow were flooding into Singapore:

> ... the refugees who came to Singapore yesterday number 275, men, women and children.
>
> Of these many are whole families and they are all native Roman Catholics from up-country in the Swatow district, which has been over-run and devastated by Chinese Reds or Bolsheviks. They are absolutely destitute, and Father [Stephen] Lee, who is working at the Chapel all by himself, is housing and feeding them and is arranging for their employment as soon as possible. Many of these refugees are farmers.
>
> What is surprising is that this is the fourth batch of refugees to arrive in Singapore from the same district, all of whom are Roman Catholic converts. The first batch arrived here on February 4 and consisted of 90 people, the second on February 18 and numbered 375, the third on February 25 of whom there were 40, and, as we have seen, the fourth yesterday. And the end is not yet, as there is another batch of about 300 waiting at Swatow to be sent to the Straits, while there is a constant stream of the same class crowding into the Roman Catholic Mission at that port.[5]

During a dinner conversation with Cyprian, I learnt that among the Catholic refugees from Peknay (*Bailingcun*, or Bethlehem in Mandarin) who arrived in Singapore in 1928, some who were fishermen went to Aukang.[6] While some refugees eventually ended up in Malacca, and formed the Catholic village called Air Salak, others ended up in Bukit Timah or Mandai, and some settled in Kangkar, at the Aukang and Punggol area near the Church of the Nativity.[7]

To me, these accounts collectively lead to a reasonable and logical explanation. The Catholic Church was an institution that provided a variety of important services, like religious salvation, welfare, and education. A virtuous cycle arose. And when Catholic Teochew refugees came to Singapore, to avoid a troubled China, several groups ended up in Aukang and Punggol. Those who settled down, in turn, became a part of the burgeoning Teochew and Catholic community, of which the Church and the education it provided continued the virtuous cycle.

And talking about education, when it comes to Aukang, one cannot talk about its history without referring repeatedly to Montfort School.

Montfort School (1916–Present)

A primary school pupil from Holy Innocents' English School in the 1950s. Photo by the late Harold Arozoo; courtesy of Edmund M Arozoo.

According to Lynn Seah's *The Story of Montfort, 1916–2016: Age Quod Agis (2016)*, Montfort started as a single class of students in rural Upper Serangoon in 1916.[8] The class, taught in English, operated on the upper floor of a two-storey building next to the church in Upper Serangoon. (The building still exists today.) It developed into Holy Innocents' English School, Montfort School's predecessor. A Chinese class on the lower floor grew to become another full-fledged school, today's Holy Innocents' High School.

While the school building was originally the brainchild of Father Laurent—the parish priest of Serangoon—he never lived to see it completed as he was called up to serve in World War I (1914–1918) and he was unfortunately killed in action in Europe. His successor, Father Henri Duvelle, finished building the school.

The historic building next to the Church of the Nativity.

Father Duvelle, interestingly, started the Chinese class first and then an English one, engaging Mr Lee Ah Kow to teach the English class which ran until 1919 when most of the students completed Standard 2, equivalent to about Primary 3. With hardly any students remaining, Mr Lee Ah Kow left.

Father Duvelle's successor as parish priest of Serangoon was Father Edward Becheras, who recruited a teacher upon finding 30 students in March 1920. Father Becheras was a Teochew-speaking French missionary priest widely known and credited for the founding of Catholic High School in 1935.[9] He picked up Teochew precisely because he was serving in Aukang.

Mr PA D'Costa became Holy Innocents' English School's first headmaster, helping Father Becheras run the school from 1922 to 1936. Under their leadership, the school grew steadily. Soon, the building became too small to accommodate the growing number of students. Father Becheras managed to raise enough funds to add two blocks to the original school building, the first in 1927 and the second in 1929.

In 1934, Father Becheras was posted to a church in Queen Street, and Father Moses Koh took over as the parish priest of Serangoon and director of the school. As the school had grown to a size where the priest was having difficulty managing it on top of his work at the parish, Bishop A Devals, the head of the Diocese (the Bishop of Singapore and Malaya), approached the Brothers of St Gabriel about taking over the running of the school. The Brothers were then running several thriving schools in Siam.

They agreed to run the school, and in November 1936, Brother Gerard Majella from Assumption College in Bangkok arrived in Singapore. Shortly after, Brother Adolphus (later known as Father Francis Tessier) and Brother John de Breboeuf, two Gabrielite Brothers who had finished their training in London, also reached Singapore's shores.

Brother Adolphus recorded his first impressions of Serangoon:

> The road was narrow, and on both sides, large plantations of coconut trees could be seen. Only a few attap huts were visible from the road. As we drew closer to the parish church, however, more houses appeared, and around them, lots of children were playing.[10]

The Brothers of St Gabriel officially took over the management of Holy Innocents' English School from the parish in December 1936. Brother Majella became the first

Brother Director of the school. After a few leadership transitions, in 1939, Brother Noel Berthomieu arrived, bringing the number of the Brothers at the school to four (Brother Louis Gonzaga, Brother Guy Stanislaus, Brother Adolphus, and Brother Noel himself).

This peaceful existence was soon threatened by the Second World War. In 1940, the French government called up its citizens in the region to protect its interests in Indochina against the Japanese. Brother Guy and Brother Noel were enlisted. In 1941, the school was requisitioned by the Australian Imperial Force (AIF) for the war effort. Subsequently, Singapore fell to the Japanese in February 1942. As a result, Brother Adolphus and Brother Vincent, who were Canadian natives and British subjects, were interned by the Japanese in Changi Prison. Brother Guy, who had contracted tuberculosis when he was in Indochina, succumbed to the illness in May 1942. Only Brother Louis and Brother Noel were left to run the school with about 10 teachers.

Incidentally, it was in Changi Prison that Brother Vincent shared his vision of a boys' home with a fellow prisoner, Australian philanthropist William T. McDermott.[11] From their shared experience of the War, the two kind-hearted souls realised Boys' Town in January 1948. It offered both a home and hope for boys who were orphaned, displaced, poor, or troubled.

At the end of 1943, the Brothers were notified that their services were no longer required at the school. They joined a group of Eurasians and Chinese Catholics who were being resettled by the Japanese in Bahau, Negri Sembilan, Malaya. The Bahau Settlement was part of a scheme to ease the food shortage in Singapore by moving people to places where they could farm. Unfortunately, about 800 of the 3,000 settlers died from malnutrition and malaria.

When the Japanese Occupation ended in September 1945, Brother Louis Gonzaga returned to Singapore and rallied the former teachers, and primary classes were restarted at Holy Innocents' English School in October 1945. Secondary classes reopened in January 1946. In 1948, more Brothers arrived to augment the work of the Order in Singapore. In that same year, there was an addition of a second floor to the five-classroom block along Upper Serangoon Road. The extension was opened by Sultan Ibrahim of Johor, who had donated generously to the school building fund.

In 1957, a new wing was built with two Science laboratories, a school hall, a new canteen, additional classrooms, modern sanitation, and a new field. Holy Innocents' High School moved to a new building down the road in that same year, so Holy Innocents' English School was able to occupy its vacated premises, which provided some relief to the space crunch.

Artist's impression of the aerial view of Montfort School and the Church of the Nativity in the 1960s.

However, as there were still not enough classrooms for Holy Innocents' English School, a third floor was added to the school buildings in 1959. In the same year, Holy Innocents' English School was renamed Montfort School, a name chosen to honour St Louis Marie Grignion de Montfort, whose efforts to educate youths are carried on by the Brothers of St Gabriel.

Shortly before the school was renamed Montfort, a prominent Aukang personality attended the school. He was Ng Kah Ting, the youngest Member of Parliament of Punggol (in this case referring to Aukang and Punggol) from September 1963 to August 1991.[12] In 1963, the first General Election was held, and he was elected—the youngest Member of the Legislative Assembly at only 23 years old. He was Honorary Adviser to the Public Utilities Board Daily Rated Employees' Union (1985–1989), and was conferred the Public Service Star (Bar) in 1990.

When he was a child, Ng Kah Ting lived along Punggol Road, near Punggol Village Market, and because his father wanted him to learn English, he ended up in Holy Innocents' English School.[13] Many years later, when he was a teacher at Tampines School, he worked with local community leaders and helped in the main reception committee for Prime Minister Lee Kuan Yew when he visited Punggol constituency on 2 June 1963. Shortly after the visit, Ng was asked to be a PAP candidate in the September 1963 elections, and he requested to stand in Punggol. He went on to serve the community for almost three decades (seven consecutive terms).

In fact, throughout its long history, Montfort produced a range of talented personalities who contributed much to Singapore. Other prominent alumni of Montfort included former Ministers Lim Boon Heng and Lee Boon Yang, Members of Parliament Ng Kah Ting and Augustine Tan, MINDEF Chief Defence Scientist Quek Tong Boon, Catholic Archbishop William Goh, and Olympic badminton player Derek Wong.[14]

Many of the prominent alumni of Holy Innocents' English School and Montfort School were residents of Aukang and much ink has been spilled on them.

But one less well-known name stood out for me.[15]

Catholic Teochew Benedict Teo Kah Leng (1909–2001), an Aukang resident and former pupil of the former Holy Innocents' English School, later served Montfort as teacher and principal from 1927 to 1969.[16] In 1959, when Holy Innocents' English School was renamed Montfort School, Teo became the principal of its primary section, remaining in the post till 1964.

He was also one of Singapore's pioneer poets, along with his brother Paul Teo Poh Leng. Unfortunately, his older brother Peter Teo Kee Leng and Paul, the youngest, were killed by the Japanese during the Japanese Occupation. Benedict Teo only fortunately escaped because he was visiting a friend elsewhere.[17] He wrote about his grief in a poem, "I Found A Bone", published in the school magazine. His prose and poetry were published especially during the 1950s and 1960s, up to his retirement, with 26 poems appearing in *Young Malayans* and the Montfort annual. Benedict Teo's writing style reflected that of a dedicated and thoughtful teacher-poet who saw pedagogical value in reading and writing poetry, which could teach pupils basics about English skills including pronunciation, and important values in life.[18]

Benedict Teo Kah Leng was also a devout Catholic, attending mass daily, singing in the choir at special occasions, and even serving occasionally as lector and warden at Sunday masses.[19] He also served in Catholic organisations such as the St Vincent de Paul and St Joseph's Dying Aid Association. The latter Association (also known as the Lim Zong Huey, or literally "nearing the end society") was originally founded in 1924 by devout parishioners, and officially inaugurated on 13 February 1926, with Holy Innocents' Chinese Boys' School as its office, and Father Becheras as its first Spiritual Director and Goh Lye Khiam as its first elected President. It aimed to spiritually and financially support the dying and their families; Teo was a member and served as a trustee for the St Joseph's Dying Aid Association, which was located in close proximity to Montfort. Many Catholic Teochews were members.[20] The Association often conducted Catholic prayers in Teochew; after my paternal grandmother died in 2012, Catholic prayers in Teochew were recited over her casket at her wake.

Quite clearly, Teo was an exemplary Montfortian, dedicated to his faith and education.

In 1961, another Montfortian milestone was reached when the school introduced its first pre-university class, which was co-ed. In 1975, pre-university classes were transferred to Catholic Junior College.

With Montfort School having classes all the way from Primary 1 to Pre-University 2, in 1974, the primary school section was separated from the main school and became Montfort Junior School, with Mr John Wee Bak Hoe appointed the school's first principal. Brother Albert became the principal of the secondary school.

A Kangkar boy who attended both Montfort Junior and Secondary from 1974 to 1983, shared his memory with me:[21]

> I grew up a Montfort Junior and Secondary, and Catholic Junior College, boy. Growing up in a kampong dominated by Catholics and having attended English Catholic School, I grew up knowing more about Catholics than my own religion which is a mixture of Buddhism and Taoism.
>
> During my time, there was a Montfort School teacher called Mr Peter Tan, who eventually moved to Maris Stella later. He played the guitar very well. He was also the band master... I wanted very much to be in the band, because that was the only way I could learn and attend sunrise mass at the Church of the Nativity. Those were memorable years.

Father Augustine Tay, who attended Montfort School, recalled playing at the house of his classmate Ali Bin Abdullah.[22] After a whole day of climbing trees and eating rambutans, Ali's mother would call out to them in Teochew—even though she was Malay—and ask them to drink her home-brewed cooling tea, made of Chinese herbs, to help combat the "heatiness" of rambutans—a very Chinese concept.

The evolution and history of the missionary brothers' involvement in the school landscape at Aukang (and later Hougang) were reflective of the evolution of the area. Foreign brothers led Montfort before locals took over. My father once reflected, "Similarly, this can be seen from the photographs of the Principals of St Gabriel's, in a sense. The earlier photographs are of European missionaries, the later ones show local missionary brothers, and the ones closer to the present show laymen. So there has been a change over time."

This recognition of the immense contributions of the Gabrielite Brothers has been shared by generations of Montfortians. Montfort alumni Tai Wei (1993 to 2002) reflected upon his time at Montfort:

> Montfort has a strong ethos established by the Gabrielite brothers. They made a conscious decision to stick to their values and not chase school rankings and reputation. Back then, many prominent folks came from Montfort, such as Cabinet ministers like Mr Lim Boon Heng or the GIC Group Chief Investment Officer Mr Ng Kok Song. I think this was because back in the day it was the only good English school in the area…
>
> But Montfort was, and remains, a really good school. The focus was always on education, personal development, and being benevolent and kind. In my CCA, the National Police Cadet Corps (NPCC), we really had fun. It was all about the development of the boys. We pushed our boys hard. Tough love. We often said it was like training for National Service (NS). Many went on to do very well in National Service, with a good number being commissioned as Officers. I had many fond personal memories of my CCA and how the morale was high and school spirit was strong. The Montfort boys that I knew were rugged and resilient.
>
> I eventually became an officer during NS and later even won a Government scholarship to Stanford.
>
> Sometimes, I can't imagine how far I have come. Upon reflection, I guess I lived up to the school motto of *Age Quod Agis*.

One person who exemplified the deeply intertwined and shared history between Montfort School and the Church of the Nativity was Madam Maria Lee Kin (1901–1990), known affectionately as "Tor Lee Kou" (literally translated as "religious instruction auntie") or "Ah Kou" (auntie), probably Singapore's most famous catechism teacher.[23] Despite the fact that she was held in awe and fear, Montfortians of her era—who studied in the school between the late 1940s and the early 1980s—remembered her fondly as she was a local legend.

Many years on, sharing his memory of Tor Lee Kou on Facebook in 2016, retired educator and former Republic of Singapore Air Force (RSAF) pilot Joseph Tan who was in Primary 6 in 1964 and completed his 'O' levels in 1968 wrote:

> Yes, indeed, I remember "Tor Lee Kou" who taught catechism in Teochew when I was in Primary school at Montfort from 1959 to 1964. She prepared me for the Sacrament of Penance and Holy Eucharist at The Church of Our Lady of Nativity located next to Montfort. Thankfully, it was smooth sailing for me as I could memorise all the required prayers in Teochew! She complimented me to my mother but my elder sister had a hard time with her and she literally left her Teochew catechism for English catechism.[24]

Beyond teaching catechism in Teochew, often instilling the fear of God in the young souls under her charge, Tor Lee Kou also travelled throughout Aukang to visit and console the sick among both Catholics and non-Catholics, and doing missionary and social work.[25] She also took the initiative to look after Our Lady's Shrine in front of the Church of the Nativity, performing the task faithfully every day until she left the parish. She was taken seriously ill after more than 45 years of work in the church, and after her recovery, left Aukang to stay with the Little Sisters of the Poor at Thomson Road. She passed away on 9 June 1990. To pay tribute to her devotion to her faith, her legacy to Montfort, and her contributions to the Church and larger society, the 1990 Montfort annual duly published an obituary on her passing.

From a dinner chat with Bryan Goh, I learnt that Tor Lee Kou was likely a Teochew from Peknay, and that was why her Teochew was slightly different from other varieties of Teochew. Cyprian Lim observed that there were many shades of Teochew spoken then and today, with different accents corresponding to different places of origin.[26] Just like Hokkien, Teochew was a variation of the Minnan language.

During my conversation with Cyprian mentioned earlier, I understood the background of the devoted and dedicated Peknay Catholic Teochews. At the time,

I rushed home to discuss this finding in greater detail with my father.

"Were you ever taught by Tor Lee Kou? And did you find her Teochew odd?" I asked.

My father replied, "Of course, I was taught by Tor Lee Kou! After all, I was a student at Holy Innocents' English School from 1953 to 1959."

He then reflected, and replied, "And now that you mention it, her Teochew was a bit odd. There were some words that we did not understand. Also, she had a slightly different intonation. But now it seems we understand much better why she was such a devout Catholic! We learn new things every day."

He then leaned towards me and said, "From 1964 to 1973, I was an educator at Montfort School, teaching subjects like English and Music.

"In the 1960s, some *seng hu* (priests) from the Church of the Nativity came over to Montfort and encouraged Catholic teachers to become catechists. It was not difficult to do so, because there were prescribed texts, often referred to as the penny catechism. For example, there were lessons like—Why did God create you? And the answer was that God created me to know Him, to serve Him in this world, and to be happy with Him forever in the next.[27] Well, at least, this was one of the lessons I could remember. So, I was a *Tor Lee Chek* (religious instruction uncle)!"

Well, we learn new things every day.

The Church of the Nativity of the Blessed Virgin Mary (1853–Present)

The Church of the Nativity of the Blessed Virgin Mary is Singapore's third oldest Roman Catholic church, after the Cathedral of the Good Shepherd (1832) and St Joseph's Church (1851).[28]

In 1853, when tigers roamed freely about the gambier and pepper plantations of Upper Serangoon, there were only 40 Teochew converts who lived with their Catholic priest, Father Ambrose Maistre, of the Paris Foreign Missions.[29] (To be spared from these tigers must have been an oft-repeated prayer of Fr Maistre.) A hundred years later in 1953, the Church of the Nativity at the seventh-and-a-half milestone Upper Serangoon was reportedly more than 6,000 strong, and no longer were tiger-related prayers uttered by the congregation. But one particular prayer must have resonated many times in the church—the Hail Mary:

The Church of the Nativity of the Blessed Virgin Mary today.

> Buan hock Ma Li Ah
> Muah pee siah thong chia
> Chu erh jer kai yan
> Nng tang jer wee charn mui
> Jer tai cher Ya Sou
> Peng wee charn mui
> Thian chu siah boh Ma Li Ah
> Wee ngor teng chuey jin
> Kim khi thian chu
> Kip ngor teng si how.
> **Amen.**

This is the story of the "Nativity Church", "Aukang Church", or "Montfort Church", which grew from humble origins serving a small rural community to a significant, gazetted national monument (in 2005) today.

Originally a tiny attap chapel built in 1853, it was subsequently replaced by a brick chapel and called St Mary's Chapel.[30] Both of these historical structures bore no resemblance in external architecture to the current church.

By 1896, only a few decades later, there was a great increase in the numbers of Catholics in Serangoon, and so there was a need to build a larger church.[31]

Father Jean Casimir Saleilles, parish priest from 1881 to 1911, was responsible for building the present church in 1901. He named it the Church of the Nativity of the Blessed Virgin Mary. Fr Saleilles was known to be hands on with the construction work. For example, he personally raised the new, heavy, brass bell to the belfry with a rope by himself.[32] Father Charles Nain from Burgundy in France, and who was another MEP priest, was tasked to design the architecture of the new church.

One of the Church's most memorable story is from the Japanese Occupation, when a bomb fell at its doorstep but never detonated.[33] While houses and land around the church were devastated during the War, the church remained unscathed.

Father Francis Chan (parish priest from 1946 to 1955) erected the Shrine of St Anne and the Shrine of St Francis Xavier in the compound behind the sacristy. His good relationship with Sultan Ibrahim of Johor led the Sultan to present the Church with the statue of the Immaculate Conception of Mary in 1947.[34] The Sultan donated the marble statue to the church as a token of his friendship with Fr (later, Bishop) Chan.[35]

Catholicism in Aukang (1853–Present)

In Aukang, Catholic faith and Teochew traditions were combined. For example, Catholic convert Angeline Yeo (born 1942) shared her experience of how she combined the Chinese marriage practice of giving *Si Dian Jin* (four items of gold) to her daughters-in-law, but instead of giving them traditional jewellery, they received a crucifix and a rosary ring.

> My family had a provision shop directly opposite Nativity Church but I wasn't a Catholic. We stayed at a house just behind the shop. In 1969, I converted because I got married to a Catholic. My Mother-in-law was very old fashioned and didn't like marriages of mixed religion. I was a Buddhist before that, but we never really followed the religion. Also, I felt that it would be better if I just followed my husband's religion. Moreover, I had to convert or else we couldn't get married in Church. At that time, I did not want to go against the church rules, so I just followed my husband. My mother was insistent on Teochew family traditions, she asked for the typical four types of gold—usually a golden necklace with a pendant would consist of two things and then either a bracelet or anklet followed by a ring. My mother-in-law gave me a pair of earrings and a necklace and pendant. When I had my own daughters-in-law, I changed the practice a little bit. I still gave them the four types of gold, but the pendant would be a crucifix, and the ring was a rosary ring.

Angeline Yeo also shared about her experiences at the Church of the Nativity, where catechism and mass were conducted in Teochew:

> When I converted, I had to go for one-to-one Catechism with a lady we called Fatty Ng [sic]. She was a teacher in a school and taught Catechism in Teochew before I was baptised. We were taught Teochew prayers for a year, about two times a month. From the moment I converted, I worked for the church until now. During my time in church, I think my faith became stronger than my late husband's faith, because I truly experienced God's love through the priests. Fr Berthold married us in church. He was nice and welcoming towards me, especially because he was close to my husband's family. After I converted, I worked for the church, sweeping the church, and

> the priests would always give us fruits and snacks. Two years after I converted, Fr Matthias Tung started the Teochew choir, of which I was the pioneer batch. My goodness, Fr Tung's Teochew was a mishmash of Hokkien and Singlish and English. He was not very fluent in Teochew, but he wanted to have Teochew Mass for the Teochew people. Sometimes the other priests would help to celebrate mass in Mandarin—Fr Peter Lu and Fr Jeannequin—and we would answer in Teochew.
>
> The priests always put the people first. They would attend all our meetings and go to people's houses. They would show us all kindness. I think that is why Aukang people are always known for being pious and warm-hearted, because we were taught well by the priests. Eventually, people used to refer to the cemetery next to the church as the "holy land of Singapore". When we exhumed the cemetery for re-development, there were quite a few perfect bodies, non-decomposed. So many of us witnessed the exhuming and were amazed at the bodies still intact, people said it truly was a holy land. Also, people said it was a holy land because we have the most number of seminarians and most number of jubilees celebrated in our church. Many people, after seeing the examples set by the priests, all wanted to join the seminary.
>
> Now, even though I'm nearly eighty years old, I still continue my service to the church in whatever way I can.[36]

The strong faith of the Catholics of Aukang even influenced some non-Catholics who lived in the area. One such example was Frankie Choo, who stayed at Kampong Sireh, on the outskirts of Aukang. He was a Taoist and his grandmother ran a Taoist temple called the Mah Cho Keng. Yet he still made many Catholic friends at Aukang and frequented the Church of the Nativity and the surrounding areas. Frankie Choo referred to the Church of the Nativity as "Montfort Church", because many of his friends from Montfort attended that church. He recalled that:

> Montfort School and Montfort Church [sic] were very big, my friends and I used to play catching at the cemetery at the church. Last time, we were not scared of ghosts—we were more excited if we saw one!

> I remember the statue of Mary the most, because my friends would always go and say prayers at the statue when they reach, and before they go home. At first, I made fun of them saying they were scared of ghosts and were asking Mary for protection and thanking her after that. Later on, they told me they were just praying for their families and friends. I was very surprised because most people who came to my grandmother's temple only prayed for themselves. I even asked them to pray for me.[37]

Catholic Teochew Agnes Chan shared her story with Bryan Goh on 6 January 2017 as he was writing his thesis for the Department of History at the National University of Singapore. As a child, Agnes stayed at Lorong Santun, next to the Church of the Nativity. Her entire family was Catholic and her father worked for the Europeans as a labourer.

Agnes later became a mother of 11 and a grandmother of 17. She was so inspired by her mother's Catholic faith that she brought her children up in the same faith, and they became in turn active members of the various churches in the Serangoon area. Agnes said that she regularly attended Teochew Mass at the Church of the Nativity on Saturdays. She said:

> Even now when we go for confession, the priest would immediately know we are from Aukang because a whole generation of Aukang Catholics learnt to pray the same prayer in Teochew.[38]

Catholic Teochew Lynn Delphine Lim, who was born and grew up in Aukang, and attended CHIJ Ponggol when she was schooling, lived just opposite the Church of the Nativity. She shared more about Catholic prayers in Teochew, including how many in her family were part of the St Joseph's Dying Aid Association:

> My family and I were all deeply involved in church activities in our growing up years. My brothers were both altar boys and my older brother and I were all in the choir.
>
> In those days, the Teochew prayers were all taught to us by my paternal grandma. We learnt them when we were just kids. Now, I can only remember the "*buan hock Ma Li Ah*", the Hail Mary, by heart.

> There was a long set of prayers, and later on there was a "Romanised book" we use now, like "*hanyu pinyin*". We would recite these Catholic prayers when someone passed away, on the 7th day, 100th day, and so on.
>
> My grandma, who has already passed away, and my mum and dad are all members of the St Joseph's Dying Aid Association at the Nativity Church. They devoutly say prayers for the deceased almost nightly, as long as the dead person is a member of the association and the family bought the casket from the association.
>
> A bus will take them to these places, sometimes as far as Jurong. These people were likely Catholic Teochews so they wanted Teochew prayers to be recited nightly during the wake. And sometimes there are several places to go to, even during festive seasons like Christmas and Chinese New Year, they will still go. My mum is still doing so.[39]

Clearly, the Catholic Teochews at the Church of the Nativity had a strong sense of faith and inspired others in the same light, even till today. Most of the construction work done in the church was funded by fundraisers carried out by the congregation, because of their love for the Church.[40] As Agatha Koh wrote in 1984:

> It is precisely this regard that the people of the parish have for this landmark of Hougang that has led to a plan to refurbish and renovate it…
>
> There could still be a copper bell tower, but that depends on how much money can be raised. But whatever changes are wrought, some things will be the same.
>
> The parishioners have decreed that the vaulted ceiling, which gives the church so much of its character, remains.

Nevertheless, the Church was not immune from changes from development. It was reported in *The Straits Times* on 4 August 1986 that:

> The Government is exhuming 2,300 graves at the Church of Our Lady of Nativity Cemetery at Holy Innocents Lane, off Upper Serangoon Road.[41]

Catholicism in Aukang (1853–Present)

Some of the niches were eventually reinterred at Mandai Columbarium.[42]

The church catered not only to spiritual needs, but social needs as well. At one point, there were a total of four schools within the church compound: Montfort Secondary School, Holy Innocents' Primary School for boys, Holy Innocents' (Chinese) Girls' School for the primary level, and the Convent of the Holy Infant Jesus (CHIJ) primary school.[43] Today, the only school standing in its grounds is the Nativity Church Kindergarten.

Located next to the Church today is CHIJ Our Lady of the Nativity, originally known as CHIJ Ponggol, established in 1957 in Punggol to serve the needs of girls in the area.[44] It was renamed in 2001, and while the new building was completed in 2001, it was officially opened on 28 May 2004.

Today, CHIJ Our Lady of the Nativity stands at the site of the former Montfort School.

Endnotes

1. Marc Rerceretnam gave a talk on this topic at a Peranakan Association event held at NUS Baba House on 25 May 2019.

2. Melody Zaccheus, "Teochew Immigrant's Role in Founding Catholic High", in *The Straits Times*, 22 May 2019.

3. Bryan Goh, "The Catholic-Teochew Rhythm: Communal Identity in Hougang, 1945–1981", *Sojourn: Journal of Social Issues in Southeast Asia*, Vol. 33, No. 1 (March 2018), pp. 227–264.

4. For a first-hand account, you can listen to Brother Emmanuel's oral interview with Rosie Marie Chng (Accession Number 001739; recorded on 29 April 1996).

5. Malaya Tribune, "Refugees from Swatow", in *Malaya Tribune*, 27 March 1928, p. 7.

6. Cyprian learnt this from Dr Clement Liew, a local church history researcher.

7. This section is based on Cyprian Lim, *My Maternal Roots: A Story of Family, Faith and Freedom* (Singapore: Genealogy Society Singapore and World Scientific, 2019), p. 133.

8. The section on the history of Montfort School is largely based on Lynn Seah, *The Story of Montfort, 1916–2016: Age Quod Agis* (Singapore: The Straits Times Press, 2016). It is also based on other sources, cited separately. Special thanks must also go to Montfort Alumni.

9. Melody Zaccheus, *op cit*.

10. Lynn Seah, *op cit*.

11. This paragraph is based on http://history.catholic.sg/the-brothers-of-st-gabriel-sg/. Accessed 10 April 2019.

12. This section is based on Punggol Community Club, *Punggol Community Club (Official Opening) Souvenir Magazine*, 13 March 1993, Singapore, p. 9.

13. Ng Kah Ting, cited in Lynn Seah, *op cit*.

14. As cited by Lee Hsien Loong, in his speech at Montfort School's Centennial Fundraising Dinner on 9 April 2016.

15. Thanks to Robert Yeo bringing my attention to this amazing gentleman.

16. This section on Benedict Teo Kah Leng's life is based on Eriko Ogihara-Schuck, "Teo Kah Leng's Malayan Poetry", in Teo Kah Leng, *I Found A Bone and Other Poems* (Singapore: Ethos Books, 2016), pp. 11–30.

17. His brother's life story is covered in a later section on the Punggol massacres.

18. Eriko Ogihara-Schuck, "Editor's Introduction", in Teo Kah Leng, *op cit*., p. 8.

19. This section on Benedict Teo Kah Leng's life is based on Eriko Ogihara-Schuck, "Teo Kah Leng's Malayan Poetry", in Teo Kah Leng, ibid., pp. 11–30.

20. Personal communication with John Liow, who shared his reflections and memories of St Joseph's Dying Aid Association (SJDDA) with me, on 11 December 2019. For the history of the SJDDA, do visit https://dyingaid.org/history/.

21. Interview with S. Lim.

22 This story recounted by Father Augustine Tay was cited in Bryan Goh's "Hougang: Diversity in a Teochew Enclave", in *Muse SG*, No. 38, Vol. 11, Issue 02, p. 8.

23 This section is based on the 1990 Montfort annual, "In loving memory: Madam Maria Lee Kin (1901–1990)".

24 Joseph Tan's personal account, kindly shared with the author.

25 This paragraph is also based on the 1990 Montfort annual, *op cit.*

26 This observation is based on Cyprian Lim, *op cit.*, p. 101.

27 This penny catechism was also recited by Brother Emmanuel in an oral interview with Rosie Marie Chng, *op cit.*

28 Nicholas Yeo, "The Church of the Nativity of the Blessed Virgin Mary: 160 years and counting", in *The Lion Raw*. Source: https://lionraw.com/2012/01/16/385/. Updated 16 January 2012. Accessed 6 July 2019

29 This paragraph is based on The Straits Times, "They used to pray: spare us from tigers", in *The Straits Times*, 2 August 1953, p. 3.

30 This paragraph is based on the Church of the Nativity of the Blessed Virgin Mary, "History of the Church". Source: http://www.nativity.sg/index.php/history. Updated 2016. Accessed 2 July 2019. It is also based on Cheow Sue-Ann, "Sultan's gift holds significance for church", in *The Straits Times*, 19 October 2017.

31 The Straits Times, "Roman Catholic Chinese", in *The Straits Times*, 22 January 1896, p. 2.

32 Bernard Bradberry, cited in Cheow Sue-Ann, *op cit.*

33 Ibid.

34 This paragraph is based on Cheow Sue-Ann, *ibid.*

35 Ibid.

36 Excerpts from an interview conducted on 9 January 2017 by Bryan Goh for his thesis, "The Rhythms of a Catholic-Teochew Community: Church, Family and School in Hougang (1945–1981)", for the Department of History, National University of Singapore, AY2016–2017.

37 Excerpts from an interview conducted on 11 January 2017 by Bryan Goh for his thesis, ibid.

38 Excerpt from an interview conducted on 6 January 2017 by Bryan Goh for his thesis, ibid.

39 According to personal communication with Lynn Delphine Lim on 20 December 2019.

40 This section is based on Agatha Koh, "In a Little Parish Church", in *The Straits Times*, 9 December 1984.

41 The Straits Times, "Graves to be exhumed", in *The Straits Times*, 4 August 1986, p. 10.

42 Personal communication with Khoo Ee-Hoon, through email.

43 This section is based on Cheow Sue-Ann, *op cit.*

44 This paragraph is based on CHIJ Our Lady of the Nativity, "School History", source: https://chijourladyofthenativity.moe.edu.sg/school-information/about-us/school-history. Updated 2017. Accessed 9 September 2019.

Chapter 4
World at War (1914–1945)

The Japanese Cemetery Park entrance.

The Japanese Cemetery Park in Aukang

The history of the Japanese Cemetery Park in Hougang goes all the way to the end of the 19th century.[1] A Japanese brothel owner, Tagajiro Fukaki, donated seven acres of his rubber plantation to be used as a burial ground for destitute Japanese prostitutes who died in Singapore, called *karayuki-san* (translated euphemistically as women who have gone overseas).

During the Meiji era, many Japanese women from poor households worked as prostitutes in many places around the world, including Southeast Asia.

The British colonial government officially granted permission for the land to be used as a cemetery on 26 June 1891. Later, it was also used to bury Japanese residents who died in Singapore.

In the early years, the cemetery's graves were maintained by the Mutual Self-Help Society, which comprised mainly women from the prostitution trade. In 1915, the Japanese Association took over the running of the cemetery, with this role transferred to the Shonan Patriotic Service Association during the Japanese Occupation.

The Japanese Occupation ushered in a new phase for the cemetery, with the later tombs and memorials constructed largely to commemorate the war dead. (The cemetery was also used to bury Japanese civilians.) Even when the Occupation ended, memorials dedicated to the Japanese military occupiers were built at the cemetery.

Shortly after the war, Japanese military and civilian personnel were repatriated by the British and the cemetery was left in disuse.

In 1951, Singapore resumed diplomatic relations with Japan after the signing of the Treaty of Peace with Japan that re-established relations between Japan and former Allied nations. The Japanese government decided against removing the ashes of their soldiers from the cemetery as it was impossible to identify those that had been enshrined together. Instead, it provided funds to restore parts of the war memorials and graves in 1955.

Prostitutes, Spies, and Soldiers

Several interesting characters are buried or have memorial stones there. For example, Yoshio Nishimura (1892–1934), the Managing Director of Ishihara Sangyo Koshi Ltd., an iron ore mining company in Malaya, and President of the Singapore Japanese Society was an interesting character... and a suspected spy during the interwar period.

In December 1934, Nishimura died suddenly in the offices of the Special Branch of the police two minutes after he entered.[2] He likely committed suicide while under investigation by the Special Branch on suspicion of espionage. More than 500 people attended his funeral and over 160 wreaths were sent, occupying two lorries.

Another Japanese secret agent, Tani Yutaka (1911–1942), was commemorated in a memorial stone at the Japanese Cemetery (although the popular online perception today is that he was buried at the Japanese Cemetery). Known as *Harimau* (Malay for tiger), he passed away in a hospital in Singapore shortly after the British surrendered in 1942.

Tani Yutaka led no ordinary life.[3] He grew up in Terengganu, Malaya, where his father ran a barbershop. He had a tragic backstory: after his young sister Shizuko was raped and murdered by a violent mob, in retaliation for Japanese aggression in China during the early 1930s, he harboured a deep hatred for the Chinese and the British colonialists. Tani Yutaka then became a bandit leader operating near the borders of Malaya and Thailand, robbing trains, and stealing from wealthy Chinese and British. He was nicknamed "Harimau" precisely for his fearless and violent behaviour. Whether one views him as a Robin Hood or a bandit depends, I suppose, on one's perspective.

Japanese military intelligence agency soon noticed his exploits and recruited him as a secret agent. He provided ground information to support the Japanese invasion of Malaya in December 1941, while conducting guerrilla sabotages against the British. He died shortly after the British surrender in February 1942.

Tani Yutaka's life story has been depicted in various media, including the Japanese propaganda film *Marai No Tora* (Japanese for *Tiger of Malaya*) released in 1943 and was even referenced in a theatre play by Alfian Sa'at, "Tiger of Malaya"—which interestingly was set up as a play-within-a-play, with a Singaporean cast tasked to recreate the film in a more politically sensitive way.[4]

Parts of the propaganda film were shot on location in Singapore, such as Upper Chin Chew Street, South Bridge Road, and Orchard Road Police Station.[5] Directed by Masato Koga, written by Keizo Kimura, and produced by Daiei Film Co. in 1943, the propaganda film was deliberately filmed on location in Malaya.

The best-known military memorial is that of Field Marshal Count Hisaichi Terauchi, the Supreme Commander of Japanese Forces in Southeast Asia during the Pacific War. Terauchi, who led the conquest of Southeast Asia, was under detention at the Renggam prisoner-of-war (POW) camp in Johor when he died on 12 June 1946. He was cremated in the Japanese Cemetery and his ashes returned to Japan. A memorial, carved out from stone in Singapore and red granite from Kota Tinggi, was erected for him by Japanese Prisoners of War (POWs).

In the Japanese Cemetery Park stands the memorial of Field Marshal Count Hisaichi Terauchi, who led the occupation of Southeast Asia.

Other memorials include those dedicated to Japanese military casualties, soldiers who had committed suicide after the Japanese surrender, and those executed as war criminals. Soil from the execution grounds in Changi Prison was secretly moved by translators to the memorial site. The memorials were clandestinely constructed by Japanese POWs, transported to the cemetery and installed with a dedication ceremony attended by senior Japanese military figures on 18 May 1947.

On 30 March 1955, the Japanese government built a memorial for 135 Japanese war criminals executed in the Changi gaol for wartime atrocities such as the Sook Ching massacre. A monument for 79 war criminals who were hanged in Kuala Lumpur, Penang, and Malacca, is located next to it. In the vicinity of these stone markers is a memorial for the Japanese who died in POW camps in Singapore, Johor, and the Riau Archipelago. Japanese war veterans have also commissioned and contributed a number of memorials. They include monuments for the 4th and 5th Guards Regiments who were part of the siege of Singapore.

No one else was buried in the Japanese Cemetery since 1973 as it was among the 42 cemeteries gazetted to be closed to further burials.[6]

Today, the cemetery of more than 29,000 square metres in area and with 910 tombs, neatly laid out and harmonious with its surroundings, is often visited by Japanese students, residents, and tourists.

World War II and The Punggol Zoo

In 1942, on the eve of the Japanese invasion, the British moved their troops to the north of Singapore in preparation to fight the Japanese.[7] They needed to occupy the land on which the Punggol Zoo (also known as the Singapore Zoo) stood, so they ordered owner William Lawrence Soma Basapa (1893–1943) to close his Punggol Zoo, and gave him 24 hours to clear the area of all the animals.

However, he could not find a replacement location in such a short time. As a result, the dangerous animals like the reptiles were shot and killed, while harmless ones like the birds were released into the forest.

The zoo went on to suffer even more ignominy. When the Japanese eventually conquered Singapore, they took away the Punggol Zoo's generator and steel cages and used the land to store ordnance. Ironic then, that a place once full of life was used to store ammunition used to take lives. They also turned the site into a mess. Basapa did not outlive the Occupation, and passed away in 1943.

What the British and Japanese destroyed at Punggol during those terrible times was not just any zoo and bird park, but the original Singapore Zoo.

The massive and grand Basapa home was located at 549 Upper Serangoon Road, next to a (now demolished) private hospital, Youngberg Memorial Hospital. The Basapa home stood on more than an acre of lush ground. Basapa used his home to house a growing menagerie of wild animals and birds. One can only imagine the colours, sounds, and odours at this unique home zoo in the 1930s. The number of visitors also increased, to the point where Basapa deemed it necessary to charge a small fee to enter the grounds.

He then bought a 27-acre plot (the size of about 11 football fields) by the sea at Punggol and built the zoo and bird park there, and relocated the wildlife from his home. The park was rudimentary by present-day standards but, at the time, it was remarkable. The development included power-generation, workers' quarters, and even a bungalow on the sea for the Basapa family's weekends.

The Singapore Zoo became a major attraction for local residents and visitors, and many prominent people visited it. For example, Albert Einstein visited the zoo in 1922.[8] He was in Singapore to raise funds for the Hebrew University, but he came across "a wonderful zoological garden" which he noted down in his travel diaries.

Another prominent person to visit the zoo was Sir Percival Phillips, probably one of the greatest war correspondents in the world during the First World War. After his visit to the zoo at Punggol, Sir Percival Phillips described the scene vividly and talked about the anguish of the captured jungle animals in captivity.[9] While he clearly pitied the animals and felt for their plight, his account also provided us with a few more interesting facts.

He described the beautiful and exotic birds:

> **There were birds of all sizes, colours, and designs, some almost too foolish in appearance to be credible, like the one with a bill bigger than its body...**

He also described the animal trade taking place in the zoo.

> **Buyers come to look them over and haggle with the Indian proprietor of the camp. All are for sale. I could have bought the crocodile or the black panther at a fair price, or taken away a cobra in exchange for Straits dollars...**

And he noticed—quite rightly—that the owner of the zoo was an advocate for what we would call "marketing" today:

> Oddly enough, this strange zoo is hardly known is [sic] Singapore. Several old residents, to whom I described my visit, were almost inclined to doubt its existence. Yet the proprietor, who charged me 1s. [*author's note: this most likely refers to one Straits dollar*] to see his "guests", regards himself as a kind of local institution, and he has put up a wooden sign at the corner of the Punggol road with the inscription: "The Singapore Zoo."

Having spent a lifetime with animals and building and expanding his zoo, only to have what he loved brutally taken away from him, Basapa must have been absolutely heartbroken.

He was, in a sense, another casualty of World War II.

Today, very little is left of the once-famous and exotic zoo.[10] The skins of some of the zoo's animals were donated to the then-Raffles Library and Museum, now the National Museum of Singapore. Around 80 of these were moved to the Raffles Museum of Biodiversity Research at the National University of Singapore in the 1970s (later renamed the Lee Kong Chian Natural History Museum in 2014).

As for the land, inherited by trustees after Basapa's death in 1943, it was sold to a private investor in 1948.

Today, the site has now become part of the Punggol Promenade and no traces of it remain.

Fortifications

During World War II, fortifications dotted the north-eastern areas of Punggol.[11] They were meant to give the Allied defenders a better chance of keeping the Japanese invaders at bay—but ultimately they failed miserably. When the War ended, most of the Allied fortifications were destroyed, while some, like Fort Siloso on Sentosa, were turned into tourist attractions. Then-Member of Parliament (MP) Ng Kah Ting highlighted the neglect of the fortifications in 1988, and said that they should be restored as historical monuments. These fortifications were located at Punggol 17th Avenue and Cheng Lim Farmway 1, off Punggol Road.

In 1989, it was reported that a number of these concrete bunkers and a bomb shelter built by British troops during World War II were still standing.[12] To get to them, intrepid explorers had to trek through mosquito-infested tracks—littered with old bottles, pots, discarded planks, rotting fruit, and dead branches. From Punggol 17th Avenue, the main road, these ground-level shelters could hardly be seen. The bunkers were used as a dumping ground, according to a former resident, Mr Goh Chee Kok. There used to be orchid farms on the site, and when they were resettled the farmers threw their flower pots at the bunkers.

Bunkers and bomb shelters were definitely important in those violent days, and offered some protection against bombing raids. Robert Yeo wrote in his memoir about memories from his childhood, of military bombing raids over Aukang and a screaming air alert siren:

> There was a shelter dug near the starfruit tree in our relatively large compound where my mother breastfed me on days when the Japanese military dropped bombs. The air alert siren was terrifying and one visible reminder was the damaged doors of our house. The small splints above eye level in both sides of the wooden door were reminders of harrowing days for my parents.[13]

But bombing raids were not the only acts carried out by the Japanese during the War.

The Punggol Massacres

On the morning of 13 March 1977, 30-year-old boatel worker Peter Tan stared in disbelief when he found a human skull staring back at him from the hole he was digging on the beach off Punggol Point.[14] Then, as he looked in disbelief, he noticed yet more bones jutting out of the mud. The police were summoned, and within minutes a party from the Payer Lebar police station arrived on the scene. They quickly ordered the hole to be widened and deepened before the in-coming tide covered the spot. Several limb and rib bones were unearthed from the hole. The skull and bones are believed to be that of an adult aged between 20 and 50. The remains were later taken to the Singapore General Hospital for examination. The CID's Special Investigation Section, which deals in homicide cases, was also alerted. Initial police investigations, however, suggested that the bones might be those of a World War II victim. This assessment was because Punggol Point was one of the spots where a number of people were killed during the War. In fact, in March 1976, four skeletons were found on the beach in the same area.

Punggol Beach World War II site.

These human remains are testimony to the horrors of World War II.

Sook Ching is a Chinese term meaning a cleansing purge. The Japanese term for the operation was *Dai Kensho*, or great inspection. The massacres started shortly after the Japanese invasion of Singapore, with the Kempeitai setting up screening centres in many locations around the island.[15] One area of concentration was at Upper Serangoon Road, according to Momuru Shinozaki, a Japanese who played a prominent part in welfare activities during the Occupation. As there was a scarcity of staff in the Kempeitai at the time, men from the Hojo Kempeitai, or auxiliary Japanese military police, were picked to help dispose of the victims who were screened by the Kempeitai, as well as guard and sentry work.

If a man was suspected to be an anti-Japanese element, he would be rounded up, loaded into a lorry with many other victims, and transported to a remote location for execution. These massacres happened at many locations across Singapore, including Aukang and Punggol.

There were many eyewitness accounts of the atrocities. Cheah Aik Hang heard firing all day in Punggol in February 1942 and later saw many dead male bodies, mostly naked, floating in the sea off Punggol. His neighbour also told him that trucks were bringing Chinese males to Punggol but the trucks returned empty later.[16] Another witness, Loh Si Tang, related how he and 21 others were taken to a rubber clearing. He was fortunate, however. The Japanese guard let them go, after firing a few shots into the air. Loh had earlier been detained along with about a thousand other Chinese at Oehlers Lodge.

In 1988, farmer and community leader Mr Tan Keng Yian spoke to MP Ng Kah Ting and a group of amateur historians, that Japanese soldiers drove truckloads of young men to Punggol Beach and then machine-gunned them.[17]

Singapore lost many promising talents in the prime of their life. One of them was pioneer poet Paul Teo Poh Leng (Francis P. Ng was his pseudonym), killed by the Japanese during Sook Ching. He tragically lost his life shortly after he wrote "F.M.S.R.", a poem about a train journey from Singapore to Kuala Lumpur on the Federated Malay States Railways, inspired by T. S. Eliot's "The Waste Land".[18] Published in 1937 by Arthur Henry Stockwell of London, the poem received good reviews from luminaries at the time, such as British poet Silvia Townsend Warner and Cornish poet Ronald Bottrall. Part of F.M.S.R. first came out in the 1937 issue of *British Literary Magazine Life And Letters Today*.

Teo Poh Leng wrote way before Edwin Thumboo, long recognised as one of Singapore's literary pioneers, arrived on the scene. Unfortunately, during the War,

Stockwell's offices were bombed, leaving only a handful of copies of Teo's work in the world after his death.

So, who was this literary pioneer? Born in 1912, Catholic Teochew Paul Teo Poh Leng was the youngest sibling in a large family in Aukang. A primary school teacher, he was the brother of Benedict Teo Kah Leng, who taught at Montfort (then called Holy Innocents' English School). Benedict eventually became principal of the junior section of Montfort School.

And why was his pseudonym Francis P. Ng? Anne Teo, his niece and daughter of Benedict Teo Kah Leng, said that Francis was in fact his Catholic middle name and Ng was his mother's surname.

On a personal note, my extended family was also directly affected by the war. My father recounted that his maternal grandfather, Mr Ng, was killed by the Japanese at Punggol beach. He was one of the many unfortunate victims.

As a result, my father's grandmother had to singlehandedly raise nine children—eight daughters and one son.

A Safe Haven at Surin Lane

However, not everywhere in north-east Singapore was dangerous. Speaking with Mr Ng Yew Kang, I uncovered a safe place in war-torn Singapore: his childhood home at Surin Lane.

Mr Ng said, "I was born in 1940 and my family lived at 43 Boat Quay. In 1942, because of the impending Japanese invasion, my family moved to Surin Lane near the current Charlton Park Estate, at the fifth milestone. My family lived there for around 40 years until the house was sold by the owner to a developer, who rebuilt it into a pair of semi-detached houses.

"At the end of Surin Lane, a sloping laterite and rocky tract, was a large coconut plantation, called Keng Hong Hng. It was owned by Mr. Cyprian Lim's great-great grandfather, Mr. Paul Lee Keng Guan. The plantation extended all the way to the sixth milestone. There were many attap houses within the coconut plantation.

"Each month, there would be Malay men who came to harvest the coconuts, using a long bamboo pole with a sickle attached at the tip. The fallen coconuts were collected into big rattan baskets. The ripe coconuts (with brown husks) were de-husked, the water (juice) drained off, cut into halves, the white kennels removed from inner hard shells and dried through either being sunned or smoked. The dried kennels were exported or sold to local factories which extracted oils from the dried kennels. During those times, coconut oil was the main edible oil used for cooking by the people.

"However, what was interesting was that hardly anyone living or passing through the plantation was hit by falling coconuts, which dropped to the ground when they were ripe."

I asked, "What was the experience of those who lived at Surin Lane during the Japanese Occupation?"

Surprisingly, unlike several others, he had a different experience of the Occupation!

Mr Ng said, "Surin Lane was relatively safe from the Japanese army. This was because there was a Japanese woman who lived in a bungalow a few houses away from my family. Before the Occupation, she had married a local Chinese, a Hokkien, and was already living in the neighbourhood. I think the husband's name was Tan Koon Bee, and he was a school principal well known in Singapore.

"During the early days of the Occupation, the Japanese soldiers visited their house; the couple might have asked them not to do anything to the neighbourhood. As a result, the neighbourhood did not have any problems with the Japanese and the whole area did not suffer any atrocities.

"However, one of my uncles who was from a rich business family and lived in town was not as lucky. During the purge of wealthy Chinese, known as Sook Ching by the Japanese, he was taken and massacred by the Japanese. At the time, he was probably in his 30s. As he was from a rich family, he was targeted because many rich Chinese families in Singapore were anti-Japanese and donated towards the anti-Japanese war efforts in China before their invasion of Singapore. That was why, when the Japanese came, their first objective was to purge this group."

He leaned back, sighed, and said, "Luckily, Surin Lane remained peaceful throughout the Occupation."

Japanese Opium Dealers?

Punggol might have also been the site of illegal smuggling by the Japanese before the invasion. Mr Abu Samah bin Katoka, a 70-year-old Malay man who lived in Punggol, said that some pieces of old Qing (and some Japanese) porcelain, such as bowls, saucers, cups, and opium pipes, were dumped there by the Japanese after their surrender in 1945.[19]

He recounted how Japanese spies posed as fish dealers and built a seaside hotel at the end of Punggol Track 24 before the invasion. Mr Abu Samah, who used to live and work there as a fisherman, said the hotel sold Qing porcelain as well as common pottery to Chinese businessmen and antique collectors.

After the Japanese surrender, the Japanese demolished the hotel and smashed the Qing pottery before discarding the pieces on the beach.

He also remembered that three times a month, several large Japanese fishing boats would dock at the harbour for three days or longer, to sell their catch to Singapore fish dealers.

As 20 intact opium containers were found there, it was likely that these Japanese fish dealers could have been involved in opium smuggling.

Suffering Under the Japanese

During the Occupation, there was great suffering in Singapore. Many Chinese evacuated to Aukang, away from the city centre, to escape the war. Nevertheless, they were still affected by the invasion and Occupation.

There were many instances of rape during the first few months. Japanese soldiers raped women they could find in the village.[20] As a result, whenever the villagers heard any noises, they immediately fled in case the noises were caused by the Japanese. However, the Japanese did not enter the Church of the Nativity to rape the women taking refuge within, even though they knew they were hiding there.[21]

There were also many instances of violence and physical brutality.[22] Villagers were often slapped, especially when they did not bow to passing Japanese. Some of the Japanese soldiers used their rifle butts to hit people. They also beheaded several villagers, and the heads were paraded at the marketplace as a warning to others—but one positive side effect was that people became too afraid to commit crime.

Food was scarce and many resorted to using substitutes, which led to malnutrition. Food rationing was implemented, with ration cards given out. Phua Cheng Kew, co-owner of a bakery at Upper Serangoon Road, had been a baker since 1937.[23] During the Japanese Occupation, Mr Phua had to use tapioca powder, a poor substitute, instead of wheat flour, as supplies from Australia and Canada had dwindled. As tapioca lacked essential vitamins, people who ate the bread over a long period suffered from beriberi.

Catholic Mass for the Departed Souls

Earlier, I shared the story of Catholic Teochew Agnes Chan.

During the Japanese Occupation, Agnes' father and many of his acquaintances were unfortunately among those captured by the Japanese and murdered at Punggol End.

Because many Catholic Teochews had been taken from Aukang to be murdered, after the Japanese surrendered, the Church of the Nativity of the Blessed Virgin Mary arranged for those who lost their relatives to register the names of the dead in a small chapel at Punggol. There were many names on it. On the first day of the English calendar month, then Fr Francis Chan—before he was ordained Bishop of Penang—would lead a procession for the laity, from the Church to the little chapel singing Latin songs and praying the rosary for the dead. Upon reaching the chapel, he would celebrate a mass for the departed souls. It was a memorable ceremony for Agnes. She recalled how those ladies who were proficient in Latin hymns would lead the procession by foot all the way, refusing to sit in vehicles because they wanted to do some penance for the souls.

This was a moving recollection of a Catholic mass for the departed souls from Aukang and a poignant reflection.

Yes, we can forgive, but we must remember the past.

Endnotes

1. This section is based on the author's visit to the Japanese Cemetery Park, where there were information panels.

2. This paragraph is based on The Singapore Free Press and Mercantile Advertiser, "Funeral Of Mr. Nishimura", in *The Singapore Free Press and Mercantile Advertiser*, 8 December 1934, p. 6.

3. According to Hun Ping, Singapore Film Locations Archive, "Tiger of Malaya (1943)". Source: https://sgfilmlocations.com/2014/08/17/tiger-of-malaya-1943/. Updated 2012. Accessed 20 August 2019.

4. Cited in Akshita Nanda, "Teater Ekamatra's Tiger of Malaya presents perils of oversimplifying history", in *The Straits Times*, 20 September 2018.

5. This part is based on Singapore Film Locations Archive, *op cit.*

6. The Straits Times, "Japanese Cemetery Closed to Burials", in *The Straits Times*, 9 May 1973, p. 21.

7. This section on the Punggol Zoo (or Singapore Zoo) is based on the website, The Basapas of Singapore, "W.L.S. Basapa". Source: http://www.singaporebasapa.com/W.L.S.%20Basapa%20The%20"Animal%20Man".html. Updated 2011. Accessed 13 August 2019.

8. This anecdote on Albert Einstein is adapted from Yuen Sin, "Our Forgotten Zoo", in *The New Paper*, 18 July 2012.

9. This account is based on Sir Percival's own account in the *Daily Mail* as reported in "Sir Percival Phillips goes to Punggol", in *The Singapore Free Press and Mercantile Advertiser*, 14 January 1930, p. 18.

10. This section is based on Yuen Sin, *op cit.*

11. This section is based on The Straits Times, "Fort ruins in Punggol may be turned into tourist attraction", in *The Straits Times*, 14 June 1988, p. 1.

12. This section is based on The New Paper, "War relic turns junkyard", in *The New Paper*, 14 July 1989, p. 3.

13. Robert Yeo, *Routes: A Singaporean Memoir 1940–75* (Singapore: Ethos Books, 2014), p. 24.

14. This story is based on Paul Wee, "Macabre find at Punggol", in *The Straits Times*, 14 March 1977, p. 1.

15. This paragraph is based on The Straits Times, "All-Day Gunfire in 1942 Massacre", in *The Straits Times*, 12 March 1947, p. 1.

16. These witness accounts were reported in The Straits Times, Ibid.

17. Tan Keng Yian, cited in Gerry de Silva, "An urban Punggol tries to preserve part of its past", in *The Straits Times,* 14 June 1988, p. 19.

18. This paragraph is based on Akshita Nanda, "Work of lost Malayan poet Teo Poh Leng republished after 78 years handed to ST article", in *The Straits Times*, 12 October 2015, and Michelle Heng, "Ties that Bind: The Story of Two Brother Poets", in *Biblioasia*, 8 January 2017. Interestingly, in what is probably the only case of a transnational literary detective story centred around a poet from Aukang, Japanese scholar Dr Ogihara-Schuck, who taught American Studies and Japanese at Dortmund in Germany, flew over to Singapore to pursue her investigation into the case of the poet who disappeared. The missing poet was none other than Francis P. Ng, whose real name was Teo Poh Leng. *The Straits Times* picked up Dr Ogihara-Schuck's story and reported on it. Readers got in touch and a collaboration was later formed. And *Finding Francis: A Poetic Adventure* was published in October 2015. I am grateful, despite finding it strangely ironic how a Japanese researcher eventually found what the Japanese military hid.

19. Cephah Tan, "Duo unearth Japanese and Qing artifacts at Punggol Beach", in *The Straits Times*, 11 October 1989, p. 3.

20 Mr Lim Seng (speaking in Mandarin) was interviewed by Tan Beng Luan in an oral history recording, by the Oral History Centre (Accession Number 000089; recorded on 28 December 1983).

21 Mr Frank Tay was interviewed by Nur Azlin bte Salem in an oral history recording, by the Oral History Centre (Accession Number 003554; recorded on 23 August 2010).

22 Ibid.

23 Mr Phua Cheng Kew's story can be found in Chong Wing Hong, "Taste of life during the Japanese Occupation", in *The Straits Times*, 28 March 1985, p. 1.

Chapter 5
Memories of Gor Kor Chiok (Fifth Milestone)

Driving along Upper Serangoon one lazy Sunday afternoon, I realised that there are—and were—many different religious institutions and organisations located near or at the fifth milestone Upper Serangoon. Yes, there were many Catholic Teochews living in Aukang, but the area was diverse and complex. Some landmarks do not exist anymore, while others have evolved with the times.

Church of the Immaculate Heart of Mary

First, the Church of the Nativity was not the only Catholic Church in Aukang; for example, there was also the Church of the Immaculate Heart of Mary between the fifth and sixth milestones.

Today, the church has over 6,000 parishioners.[1] It was officially blessed and opened at Hillside Drive, Paya Lebar, by Monsignor Martin Hubert Lucas, Apostolic Delegate on 13 December 1953.[2] The church could accommodate about 500 people. All who contributed to the building of the church were invited to attend the opening.

An artist's impression of the Church of the Immaculate Heart of Mary.

The church stayed the same way until the 1970s when Fr Louis Loiseau (born in June 1926), who was in charge then (until 1981), drew up plans to build a permanent structure.³ He even started planning and fund-raising efforts to build a larger church, but eventually the project did not proceed.⁴

Tou Mu Kung Temple

Tou Mu Kung or Kow Ong Yah Temple.

Not all in the Teochew community at Aukang are Catholic. Some Taoist Teochews worship at Tou Mu Kung, sometimes referred to as Kew Ong Yah Temple (Nine Emperor Gods Temple) by the Hokkiens and Kow Ong Yah Temple by the Teochews.

The temple was built in 1921 by merchant Ong Choo Kee at the fifth milestone Upper Serangoon.⁵

One version of the backstory goes that before Ong left for Penang to strike some business deals, he knelt before Taoist deity Kew Ong Yah and promised to pray to Him for his entire life if his deals were successful.⁶ Upon achieving success, he duly acquired a talisman and housed it in his home at Lorong Chuan at an altar. This makeshift shrine was later relocated to Boundary Road near Lorong Chuan after word of his success started spreading and the shrine saw an increase in the number of devotees.

Another, likely apocryphal, story goes that there were several miners in Kuala Lumpur suffering from a deadly disease.⁷ In this version, Ong Choo Kee was a

Chinese doctor and the only one who possessed the original sacred writing of the Gods from China. Overcome by compassion for the miners' plight, he drove away the evil spirits causing death, and after that there were no more such incidents. He later founded a small temple in an attap hut.

Regardless of the temple's founding, it soon attracted many devotees. According to an unnamed old temple attendant:

> ... a rich man, Ong Chwee Tow, came to pray and was warned by the Gods that something terrible was to happen. That afternoon, a great fire razed his house to the ground.
>
> Another man, Ong Koi Gim, who had spent a great deal of money trying to get rid of a thorn imbedded [sic] in his cheek, was healed by sticking on the affected part a sacred paper obtained from the temple.
>
> These two men contributed large sums of money to the temple and a new one was built on the site on which it stands today.[8]

After Ong Chwee Tow donated a land parcel in Aukang, construction of the temple began in 1919 and was completed by 1921. Currently, Tou Mu Kung Temple is the oldest Hokkien temple dedicated to Kew Ong Yah.[9] Even though it was devoted to the worship of Kew Ong Yah, it was actually officially named after the deity's mother, Dou Mu Yuan Jun (Mother of the Big Dipper). Arguably, respect for one's and others' parents is a deeply held Chinese virtue. Dou Mu Yuan Jun is believed to hold the Register of Life and Death, which is why she is venerated by devotees hoping to prolong their lives and avoid calamities.

On the ninth day of the ninth lunar month every year, the temple holds a grand celebration to mark the end of the nine-day festival in honour of Kew Ong Yah who is believed to visit his worshippers annually. The procession's most prominent feature is the nine heavy, richly ornamented sedans in the streets meant to be manifestations of the deity's prowess and divinity. Also, nine bamboo rice measures—representing Nine Gods—are worshipped.[10]

My father had a personal anecdote relating to this exact procession.

One night, my father said, "When we lived at Jalan Lye Kwee, there would be a regular major procession starting from the Kow Ong Yah Temple, all the way up to Kangkar, at the end of Upper Serangoon Road. The end-to-end procession would be so massive that it would block traffic, which you cannot see today anymore.

Nowadays, for processions, devotees walk for a bit, and then after that they are required to take transport to their destination. In the days of old, our family would come out of our home at Jalan Lye Kwee and look at the procession.

"Ah Ma was so worried about me each time we went out to look at the procession. 'My son, you have a sharp tongue,' she would admonish. 'Please be careful. You may say something that would anger the worshippers and Kow Ong Yah. If you anger the gods, they will slap you, and your face will be slanted to one side (*meng chua*)!'"

The temple was originally designed and built in a traditional Hokkien architectural style specific to Quanzhou, Fujian.[11] The cornerstone of this style is the curvature in the roof ridges. The centre of the ridge has a blazing red pearl meant to symbolise the sun. Like many traditional Chinese temples, Tou Mu Kung was constructed with three halls—entrance, main, and rear halls. Behind the main hall there is an octagonal pagoda-like tower. The backyard has an old well that devotees use to wash their hands and faces for good luck. The temple looks like a single unit because the three halls are compacted. The main temple building is symmetrical and located at the front, while the living quarters of the temple keepers is located at the back. Two military guardian deities are painted on the doors of the main entrance.

The temple used to have a permanent stage in the forecourt, built in the mid-1920s. *Wayang*, or traditional Chinese opera performances, were held there during the celebrations of Kew Ong Yah's birth. In 1998, the stage was demolished to make room for a road-widening project. Consequently, the temple erected a temporary stage every year after that for *wayang* performances during the grand festival.

In the 1980s, there were some legal disputes over the legal ownership of the land on which the temple stood.[12] Eventually, in August 2004, the Attorney-General's Chambers appointed the Singapore Taoist Federation to manage the temple. The federation then established a committee for that purpose, which then undertook, as a first assignment, a major refurbishment of the temple because of its dismal state of disrepair.[13]

Several Teochew architectural features were adopted for its new design even though the temple's founder and land donor were Hokkien.[14] This was because there were many Teochews living in Aukang. For example, the temple's roof ridges are straighter, similar to the ones on the Teochew Yueh Hai Ching Temple.

In 2005, the temple was gazetted as a national monument.[15]

In June 2008, the temple became part of the Upper Serangoon heritage trail.[16]

Memories of Gor Kor Chiok (Fifth Milestone)

The project was known as "Colours of History, Trails of Memories", created by the Urban Redevelopment Authority. The objective was to beautify and improve the district as well as strengthen the sense of belonging among the community.

In November 2016, the committee started the restoration project to refurbish and construct extensions to the building.[17] All the refurbishments cost $6 million in total and had three phrases. The first entailed the construction of an underground carpark and a two-storey building. The second revolved around the restoration of the main temple building and the last saw the construction of a four-storey administrative block behind the temple. Today, the temple is a beautiful and significant landmark in the area.

At night, the temple looks visually stunning. Courtesy of S. Lim.

St Paul's Church

There was also a small Anglican community living in Aukang.[18] Started as a house church catering to the English-speaking community in the 1930s, St Paul's Church eventually moved into a new building in 1936, where it is still situated today.

It was the 1930s. The Great Depression was ongoing and many countries were affected, including Singapore. Rumours of war were circulating, causing an increase in members from the British and European community in the military bases scattered throughout the island.[19] It was under these circumstances that Archdeacon Graham

St Paul's Kindergarten in 1976. Courtesy of Encik Salleh Sariman.

Memories of Gor Kor Chiok (Fifth Milestone)

White, with the help of server George Rae Koehler's, had the vision of expanding the ministry of St Andrew's Cathedral to the outlying communities of Singapore.

When it was first set up, St Paul's Church started at home where a handful of worshippers met in an old mission's house of the late Mr J Gibson. This location is a stone's throw away from the present location of St Paul's Church and was later rebuilt as Sin Ming High School.

It is also currently the premises of The Helping Hand, an organisation devoted to helping ex-offenders restore their lives by helping them live in a Christ-centred fashion.[20] This helps them reintegrate into society. The house church grew quickly under the leadership of Archdeacon White and the Diocese saw the need to purchase a plot of land and build a church for the community.

Together with the land that was purchased in 1935 and the building costs donated by George Rae Oehlers, the foundation stone was laid on 3 December 1935 by Archdeacon Graham White and Bishop Basil C. Roberts.

The church was built in the design of a cross and was completed in April 1936 and dedicated to the glory of God. There is some anecdotal evidence that church services continued throughout WWII, although not necessarily in the church building itself.[21] One of the local ministers at that time, Rev Dong Bin Seng, shepherded the Church during this difficult period.

The end of the War in 1945 saw a new phase in the life of St Paul's. It took its place as an oasis of healing from the horrors of the war. The church became a food distribution centre of the Social Welfare Department.

In 1955, the vicarage and verger's quarters were completed and later that year, Rev Marrison became the first full-time priest at St Paul's Church. The priest was a pioneer who established the presence of St Paul's in Upper Serangoon. In 1961, Archdeacon DD Chelliah was appointed Vicar of the church. He was responsible for growing many of the church services for the community through the work of the Kindergarten as well as other ministries like the Sunday school, Women's Fellowship, and the Youth Fellowship.

In 1971, the church was led by Rev Simon Acland who had a soft spot for the needy and underprivileged. This led to him opening up a new session of the Kindergarten with the support of volunteer teachers, to cater for the needy students in the neighbourhood.

Soon, plans were made for a new church building and a proper church parish hall. The hall was built and dedicated in 1982 and the new church extension with the present configuration was eventually completed in 1994.

Masjid Haji Yusoff

The Muslim community in Hougang also has a place of worship at Masjid Haji Yusoff, located at Hillside Drive, near Tou Mu Kung. It was completed in 1921 and extended in September 1973.[22] The mosque was built on a "Waqf", an Islamic inalienable charitable endowment that usually involves donating a building, plot of land, or other assets for Muslim religious or charitable purposes. Ahmad bin Mohamed Salleh Angullia donated the land at the junction of Upper Serangoon Road and Hillside Drive for the building of the mosque. It later underwent redevelopment in 1995.

The mosque stands to this day in an area with many Teochews, surrounded not just by residences and businesses, but also the Tou Mu Kong temple and Catholic and Protestant churches nearby; this is symbolic testimony to how Singapore has been, and will always be, a multi-racial and multi-religious space.

Teochew Cemetery

Quite naturally, as Aukang was an area dominated by Teochews, it had a major Teochew Cemetery. This cemetery was located at the fifth milestone Upper Serangoon Road, "between Yardley Court Mansion and Ng Soon Kwee nursery".[23] It was called the Kwong Ngee Suah Teochew Cemetery and formerly belonged to the Ngee Ann Kongsi.[24]

There was an interesting discussion in the newspapers in late 1929 involving this Teochew Cemetery.

A certain L. C. Tan wrote to *The Straits Times* on 8 November 1929, calling on the Trustees of the Teochew Cemetery in Upper Serangoon Road to have sheds erected at the cemetery to shelter people who attended funerals.[25] This was useful when there was a heavy downpour or when it was a hot day. L. C. Tan went on to argue that the sheds should be built from the funds of the Cemetery Trust, if any; if not, prominent members of the Teochew community should lead a fund-raiser. He made a similar appeal through the *Malaya Tribune*.[26]

He gained support from another reader who not only congratulated him on his initiative, but who also asserted that this cemetery was the only Chinese public burial ground which did not have shelter.[27] This was important for the All Souls Day Festival, or *Cheng Meng*, to help people visiting their beloved ones' graves. Soon other readers jumped in, such as a certain C. H. Tan who commented that it was a disgrace to such a large Teochew community and called upon the trustees.[28]

But this controversy was not over. A certain member of the public G. K. M. pointed out that someone from the Teochew community had tried to build the sheds himself, but was prevented from doing so as he had no permit from the person in charge.[29] This spurred Ng Mia Yong to support G. K. M., and most memorably, Ng said that

> ... but it is not too late yet if we begin to wake up now. Bukit Brown Cemetery is clean and up-to-date, and I trust the Teochew community will try their best to follow more or less the method of management adopted there.[30]

To cut a long story short, later the sheds were built—much to L. C. Tan's gladness—and a large, tiled-roof shed was erected at the Paya Lebar end of the cemetery.[31]

Eventually, the graves were exhumed; the dead made way for the living. In 1981, the Housing & Development Board exhumed 1,000 graves from the Kwong Ngee Suah Teochew Cemetery to make way for development.[32] The other portion of the cemetery, behind the Ngee Ann Kongsi Funeral Parlour and adjacent to Liew Lian Estate, was to be exhumed later.[33] The Resettlement Department was to exhume the remains and cremate them, and relatives of the deceased were to claim the cremated remains for storage in private temples or in the HDB Columbarium at Yishun New Town, unclaimed remains would be disposed at sea.

The Lim Tua Tow Market

The Lim Tua Tow market was built before the Second World War. In 1934, the Singapore Municipal Commissioners agreed to a

> ...proposal to erect a hawkers' mart on part of the open space at corner [sic] of Upper Serangoon Road and Lim Tua Tow Road", subject to provision of funds to cover the cost estimated at $13,660.[34]

When I was conducting research for this book, I spoke to many people about the Lim Tua Tow Market, but my conversation with Mr Ng Yew Kang stood out the most.

According to Mr Ng, his family used to buy food from the famous Lim Tua Tow market. Fondly recalling his personal experiences, he told me that the market was known for selling fresh seafood, such as fresh fish, prawns, and crab. According to him, the Lim Tua Tow market and the Simon Road market were the most well-known markets in Aukang from the 1940s to 1960s, perhaps even the 1970s.

The Original Site of Da Qiao School at Lim Tua Tow Road

Da Qiao Primary School was officially opened on 11 January 1936 at North Bridge Road.[35] It was a Chinese-medium public school that served the community's educational needs, especially the needs of children from low-income families.

At the time, it was known as Tai Keou School. Tai (Da) referred to Dabu (Hakka), the province where the founder came from; Keou (Qiao) referred to Chinese immigrants in Singapore. The founder Mr Qiu Lin Rong also doubled up as the Principal of the school.

In 1939, members of the Char Yong (Dabu) Association came on board to serve as the school's Board of Directors to better support the school. Mr Yuan Ping was appointed the new Principal of the school after Qiu left. In the same year, the school shifted to Lim Tua Tow Road at Aukang. The next year, Mr Liu Jun Jie became Principal of Da Qiao Primary School.

During the Japanese Occupation, the school was closed down. After the Occupation, Mr Liu Jun Jie re-opened the school at Lorong Tai Seng in 1947. It re-located to Jalan Paya in 1964 and operated there until the end of 1980.

In 1981, Da Qiao Primary School was established as a government school in Ang Mo Kio. "Da Qiao", the Hanyu Pinyin version of Tai Keou, was chosen to perpetuate the name of Tai Keou School and recognise past contributions made to the school by members of the Char Yong (Dabu) Association. The new school started operating at 10 Ang Mo Kio St 54 in January 1982 with 38 classes and a pupil enrolment of about 1,200. The school was officially declared open by Mr Hwang Soo Jin, Deputy Speaker and Member of Parliament for Jalan Kayu on 22 July 1983. The first Principal was Mr Cheong Cheng Swee, who was later succeeded by Mrs Christina Koh in 1985, and by Mr Lee Lam Hua in 1995.

As a result of PRIME, a Ministry of Education school rebuilding programme, Da Qiao Primary moved to 8 Ang Mo Kio St 54 on 8 December 1999. The new millennium marked another milestone in the history of the school when it merged with Chong Boon Primary on 1 January 2000 to form Da Qiao Primary. The new merged school was headed by Mrs Loh Meng Har from 2000 to 2006. Mrs Bilveer Singh took over the helm as Principal from 2007 to 2013. In 2019, Da Qiao Primary merged once again with another primary school, this time Jing Shan Primary.[36]

Endnotes

1 According to the Roman Catholic Archdiocese website. Source: https://www.catholic.sg/directory/singapore_catholic_church/church-parish-information/?Ox45Q=29. Accessed 29 January 2019.

2 The Straits Times, "Church to be blessed", in *The Straits Times*, 13 December 1953, p. 9. Also see The Singapore Free Press, "A New Catholic Church", in *The Singapore Free Press*, 12 December 1953, p. 5.

3 If you are interested to read more about Fr Loiseau's life, please refer to Roman Catholic Archdiocese of Singapore, "Man of God, Man for Others—Fr Louis Loiseau", in *CatholicNews*.

4 Church of Christ the King, *Golden Jubilee: Church of the Immaculate Heart of Mary 1953–2003* (Singapore: Church of Christ the King, 2003).

5 Based on Bryan Goh, "Hougang: Diversity in a Teochew Enclave", in *Muse SG*, No. 38, Vol. 11, Issue 02, p. 8.

6 This section is based on Chow Yaw Huah and Valerie Chew, "Tou Mu Kung Temple", *Singapore Infopedia*. Source: http://eresources.nlb.gov.sg/infopedia/articles/SIP_1858_2011-12-02.html. Updated 2016. Accessed 23 July 2019. It is also based on National Heritage Board, "Tou Mu Kung Temple". Source: https://roots.sg/Content/Places/national-monuments/tou-mu-kung-temple. Updated 2016. Accessed 23 July 2019.

7 This version is best told by MT Leong, "Kew Ong Tai Tay", in *The Singapore Free Press*, 22 October 1947, p. 4.

8 Ibid.

9 This section is based on the National Heritage Board, *op cit*.

10 MT Leong, *op cit*.

11 This section is based on Chow Yaw Huah and Valerie Chew, *op cit*.

12 Ibid. This paragraph is also based on Lim, "Temple land case back in court again", in *The Straits Times*, 2 November 2001.

13 Tanya Fong, "Temple in legal tussle to be torn down", in *The Straits Times*, 19 August 2004.

14 This paragraph is based on the National Heritage Board, *op cit*.

15 Tracy Sua, "Four new heritage sites", in *The Straits Times*, 14 January 2005.

16 This section is based on the National Heritage Board, *op cit*.

17 This paragraph is based on Chow Yaw Huah and Valerie Chew, *op cit*.

18 This section is based on Bryan Goh, *op cit*.

19 Most of this section is based on St Paul's Church, "Our History". Source: http://www.st.paulschurch.org.sg/. Updated 2018. Accessed on 31 July 2019.

20 This section is based on The Helping Hand, "Our Mission". Source: http://thehelpinghand.org.sg/our-organization/our-mission/. Updated 2015. Accessed on 31 July 2019.

21 The rest of this section is based on St Paul's Church, *op cit*.

22 This section is based on Bryan Goh, *op cit*.; the Serangoon Gardens Commemorative Magazine Editorial Committee, *Serangoon Gardens: 35th anniversary, 1959–1994*, Singapore: Serangoon Gardens Commemorative Magazine Editorial Committee, 1994, p. 38; and the Majlis Ugama Islam Singapura (MUIS) website.

23 Housing & Development Board, "HDB Exhumation of Graves", in *The Straits Times*, 17 July 1981, p. 31.

24 Ibid.

25 This section is based on L. C. Tan's letter, "The Teochew Cemetery", in *The Straits Times*, 8 November 1929, p. 19.

26 L. C. Tan's letter, "The Teochew Cemetery", in *Malaya Tribune*, 12 November 1929, p. 11.

27 This section is based on TAB, "The Teochew Cemetery", in *Malaya Tribune*, 20 November 1929, p. 11.

28 C. H. Tan, "The Teochew Cemetery", in *Malaya Tribune*, 27 November 1929, p. 11.

29 This section is based on G. K. M., "The Teochew Cemetery", in *Malaya Tribune*, 11 December 1929, p. 11.

30 Ng Mia Yong, "The Teochew Cemetery", in *Malaya Tribune*, 16 December 1929, p. 5.

31 L. C. Tan, "The Teochew Cemetery", in *Malaya Tribune*, 10 April 1931, p. 2.

32 New Nation, "Exhumation", in *New Nation*, 21 July 1981, p. 2.

33 HDB, *op cit*.

34 As reported in the Malaya Tribune, "Municipal Action", in *Malaya Tribune*, 17 May 1934, p. 7.

35 Da Qiao Primary School, "The Da Qiao Story". Source: http://www.daqiaopri.moe.edu.sg/about-us/the-da-qiao-story. Updated 2016. Accessed through the Web Archive Singapore as the website does not exist anymore. It was archived by the National Library Board on 5 February 2016 and 3 September 2016.

36 Annabeth Leow, "School mergers 2019: Merry-go-round of mergers for some affected primary schools", in *The Straits Times*, 20 April 2017.

Chapter 6
Memories of Lak Kor Chiok (Sixth Milestone)

Earlier, I quoted Robert Yeo, who wrote in *Routes* that when he wanted to return home from Bras Basah Road on a bus or taxi, he would say Aukang or *Lak Kor*.[1] Ever since I worked on this book project, I had always been interested in finding out more about *Lak Kor* because, to borrow the words of a popular Singaporean phrase, it was "my father's road".

Memories of Simon Road

There is a road called Simon Road at *Lak Kor*. Well, the road is technically not named after my father, but Simon Aroozoo (1849–1931). According to Bryan Goh:

> Between Yio Chu Kang Road and the 5th milestone, the Eurasian communities resided in bungalows amidst their fruit orchards. However, the two communities did not live in mutual isolation. One site of interaction was the popular Simon Road Market at the 6th milestone. The market, frequented by both Eurasians and Teochews, was named after Simon Aroozoo (1849–1931), a Eurasian who had inherited the land from his boss, the wealthy estate owner Gan Eng Seng (1844–1899). Over time, the *Aukang-nang* label was gradually extended to these Eurasians living on the fringes, who also conversed fluently in Teochew, the lingua franca of the market.[2]

Significantly, Simon Aroozoo's grandson, prominent local educator Percival Frank Aroozoo (1900–1969) was headmaster of Gan Eng Seng School.[3] This must have delighted him immensely because of the historical and close ties the Aroozoo family had with Gan Eng Seng.

Chatting with my father's friend Lee Tong Juan, it was quite clear also that the Eurasians he personally knew from his days at Holy Innocents' English School could also speak fluent Teochew.

Other than the famous Lim Tua Tow Market near the fifth milestone, the wet market at Simon Road was very famous. Recalling his personal experiences, Mr Ng Yew Kang said, "Both markets were known for selling fresh seafood, such as fresh fish, prawns, and crab. They were the most well-known markets in the area from the 1940s to 1960s, perhaps even the 1970s. The Simon Road market was very big, and included where the current Kovan Melody condo stands."

He paused, and said, "My mother used to buy green sea turtle meat and eggs, and flying foxes there."

Serangoon English School and its Prominent Alumni

There was once a government school at Lak Kor with many students who eventually became important and prominent public personalities: Serangoon English School.

The school began life at Simon Road in 1928, housed in a two-storey building.[4] At the time, it had one headmistress, seven teachers, and seven students, and was the only government co-ed school. In 1937, three standards were added, providing students with education up to what we would call Secondary Three today. Students who successfully completed Standard Eight then went on to Raffles Institution and Raffles Girls' School respectively. In 1949, the school became a full school when the first School Certificate class offering education from Primary One to Cambridge School Certificate was formed. In 1957, the school became a secondary school and no longer had primary classes. In 1965, the first Pre-University class was formed, eventually becoming two Pre-University One classes and two Pre-University Two classes. In 1967, Serangoon English School shifted to Lowland Road and changed its name to Serangoon Secondary School. In 1976, as Junior Colleges were being established, the Pre-University section of the school was closed. In 2001, Serangoon Secondary moved again, this time to 11 Upper Serangoon View.

Mr Ng Yew Kang said to me, "Famous alumni of Serangoon English School included Mr E. W. Barker, a former Minister of Law; Mr Ngiam Tong Dow, a former Permanent Secretary of Ministry of Finance; his brother Dr Ngiam Tong Tau, who was once Director, Primary Production Department; and Mr Robert Yeo, poet and playwright."

One of the founding fathers of Singapore, Edmund William Barker was educated at Serangoon English School from 1928 to 1934. He eventually rose to become the Legislative Assemblyman (later Member of Parliament) for Tanglin in 1963, and took on roles such as Speaker of the Singapore Legislative Assembly (1963 to 1964), and Minister for Law (1964 to 1988) and National Development (1965 to 1975).

Memories of Lak Kor Chiok (Sixth Milestone)

Ngiam Tong Dow attended Serangoon English School from 1945 to 1952. He eventually attained a Bachelor of Arts (Economics, First Class Honours) from the then University of Malaya and a Master of Public Administration from Harvard University. He went on to distinguish himself in public service, for example in the Prime Minister's Office, Ministry of Finance, Trade and Industry, and National Development. His brother, Dr Ngiam Tong Tau served in the Agri-Food and Veterinary Authority of Singapore for more than two decades, rising to become Chief Executive Officer. He is recognised as the architect of modern farming and agrotechnology parks in Singapore and has been responsible for the transfer of farming technology to several countries in the region.

Prominent poet and playwright Robert Yeo also pointed out to me that Aukang produced two Commissioners of Police: Yeo's neighbour Goh Yong Hong (Commissioner from 1979 to 1992) and Tee Tua Ba (from 1992 to 1997), son of a provision shop owner in Upper Serangoon Road. The latter attended Serangoon English School from 1949 to 1959.

Tee Tua Ba eventually led a long, distinguished, and exciting police career.[5] One example of gripping excitement was when he was part of an operation to apprehend notorious kidnapper Loh Ngut Fong (aka "Ah Seng") and his gang, who were hiding out in a house off Yio Chu Kang Road. The massive operation ended in a shootout and the death of the wanted kidnapper. He was also the Officer-in-Charge of the Marine Police during the terrorist hijacking of the ferryboat Laju, off Pulau Bukom on 31 January 1974, and in a dramatic bid to win the confidence of Palestinian leader of the hijack team, he held and guided the terrorist's Browning automatic to his temple. The emotional terrorist ended up trusting him, and gave up their arms. After his retirement from the Police Force in 1997, he was Singapore's envoy to Brunei and non-resident Ambassador to Switzerland, among many other high-level appointments.

Robert Yeo also pointed out to me that Lim Choon Mong, head of the Liberal Socialist party (or Lib Soc for short), who lived at Valley Road and was a science teacher at Anglo-Chinese School, was one of the rare few who attended the constitutional talks in London in the 1950s.[6] Lim was an old boy of Serangoon English School.[7]

After Singapore was granted partial internal self-government under the Rendel Constitution in 1955, Chief Minister David Marshall led an all-party delegation to London to determine the terms of full internal self-government for Singapore in 1956. Lim Choon Mong was one of them—he was one of the members of the All-

Party Constitutional Mission to London in April 1956 (then as part of the Progressive Party). The next year, as head of the Lib Socs he was one of the members of the All-Party Constitutional Mission to London in April 1957, led by Chief Minister Lim Yew Hock. And in 1958, he once again was part of the delegation—which consisted of Chief Minister Lim, Abdul Hamid bin Haji Jumat, Chew Swee Kee, and Lee Kuan Yew—that conducted the final round of the constitutional talks in London.[8]

Mr Ng Yew Kang also shared with me about the principal who was at Serangoon English School during his time there. "At Serangoon English School, the principal Mr Peter Lim was a stern and sullen fellow. He did not tolerate any nonsense from the students. He would cane students who flouted school rules openly at the school assemblies. It was even rumoured that he had a revolver in his drawer."

It might have been apt that one of its memorable principals was a disciplinarian rumoured to have a revolver. After all, later on, the school was turned into an army camp. Mr Ng said, "Serangoon English School later moved to Lowland Road, and then to Upper Serangoon Road near the Nativity Church. The premises were turned into an army camp, and now have been developed into a condominium."

According to Robert Yeo, far more inspiring than Mr Peter Lim was another principal, Mr Low Ngiong Ing, affectionately known as NI Low.[9] While he stayed for less than a year at Serangoon English School while he was filling in for principal SC Ting who was on leave, in 1953, he transformed the school. An anti-colonialist at a time when most teachers accepted that Singapore was still a British colony, NI Low talked enthusiastically about Mahatma Gandhi's non-violent struggle to win independence from India, and even came up with a school song that was sung at assembly on occasions that did not clash with imperial commemorations.[10]

NI Low was the author of two books, **When Singapore Was Syonan-To** and *Chinese Jetsam on a Tropic Shore*.[11] Born on 6 June 1900, he came to Singapore at the age of nine, was orphaned at an early age, and—after much determination, sense of purpose, and encouragement—was awarded a Straits Settlements Government Scholarship in 1919. He then studied Arts at Hong Kong University and upon his return to Singapore, started what turned out to be a long and fruitful career in the Education Service.

He held a range of positions such as Headmaster, Assistant Director of Education, Committee Member of the Local Teachers' Association and the Singapore English School Teachers' Cooperative Thrift and Loan Society, and Assistant Superintendent of Private Schools, among others, and wrote articles on how to improve education in Malaya.[12] He was granted a certificate of naturalisation by the British in 1939.[13]

His daughter Ethel Low, who began violin lessons at the age of six under Goh Soon Tioe, one of Singapore's best known violinists, was among one of the survivors of a ship called Kuala, sunk by Japanese bombers during the War.[14] His wife was also on the same ship. After swimming for hours, they reached a small island, from which they were taken to a nearby settlement by a firewood junk, and later came back to Singapore during the Occupation.

The Stories of Joo Hong Road, Lim Ah Pin Road, and Florence Road

Near Simon Road is Florence Road, Joo Hong Road, and Lim Ah Pin Road. I'm familiar with these road names because my father is Simon and one of my aunts, Florence. During a flight of fancy, I once even speculated that my Ah Ma had named family members after these two road names.

Surely, this had to be more than a mere coincidence—but my father shot down the idea that he and his sister were named after road names. In the end, intrigued, I went about discovering who the streets were named after instead.

These are the stories of Joo Hong Road, Lim Ah Pin Road, and Florence Road at the sixth milestone in Aukang.

Joo Hong Road, located off Lim Ah Pin Road in Hougang, is named after Mr Tay Joo Hong.[15] It is near Lim Ah Pin Post Office, located at the junction of Upper Serangoon Road and Lim Ah Pin Road.

Tay Joo Hong had many businesses in Singapore and Malaysia. His house was located in the area covering Lim Ah Pin Post Office and the Esso petrol station nearby. His extended family resided at what is Joo Hong Road and Lim Ah Pin Road today.

Lim Ah Pin Road. Picture taken by the author in 2019.

The nearby Lim Ah Pin Road in Kovan was named after Montfort alumnus Larry Lim's grandfather, Peter Lim Ah Pin.

Next to Lim Ah Pin Road is Florence Road and Florence Close. As it turns out, Peter Lim Ah Pin (1890–1943) married Florence Yeo Ah Chee (1887–1962), who was formerly from Malacca, and brought up at the orphanage at the Convent of the Holy Infant Jesus at Victoria Street.

Florence Road. Picture taken by the author in 2019.

Lim Ah Pin was born in China, and came to Singapore in 1894 when he was around 12 years old. Upon arrival in Singapore, his father dealt with goods, buying and selling goods like footwear and clothing.

A diligent and enterprising worker, Lim Ah Pin took over his father's business upon the latter's death. He expanded from his grandfather's provision shop and moved into rubber; tin mining; and even the silent film industry. Eventually, he became a successful and prominent vermicelli manufacturer, and was affectionately known as the "Bee Hoon King". Lim converted to Catholicism upon his marriage and was baptised Peter.

Incidentally, James Lim Keng Hoe (born 1916) was responsible for the road being named after his father Peter Lim Ah Pin, at the time when Singapore was still a British colony.[16] He wrote to the then Rural Board, requesting that the road be named after his father, because the road had no name at the time, and tenants who were staying there found it difficult to send or receive letters.

In view of Lim's well-known generosity and philanthropy, as well as his properties along Upper Serangoon Road, the colonial government decided to name the roads after Mr Lim and his wife Mdm Yeo. And that explains the significance of Lim Ah Pin Road, Florence Road, and Florence Close in the area.

The Upper Serangoon Community Centre and Boys' Club

The Serangoon Community Centre was opened in May 1953, at Lim Ah Pin Road.[17] It engaged prominent members of the community, who served on its board, for example, Lim Choon Mong of Valley Road was President and Goh Yong Meng, formerly one of the top managers at MPH, was Secretary.[18] And it had popular dances with live bands as well, making the place young and vibrant, and these dances were supported by a wealthy merchant and construction magnate Lee Kim Tah, who lived at the fifth milestone.[19] The community centre also formed a literary and dramatic club in 1957.[20]

More importantly, the community centre had two key amenities not often found in rural areas: a library and a boys' club. The library, which opened in December 1953 and boasted a wide-ranging selection of 2,500 books, was in fact the first branch library of the Raffles Library and Museum outside the city.[21]

Next to the library was the Upper Serangoon Boys' Club, the ninth boys' club to be instituted in Singapore, which provided facilities for both indoor and outdoor games, and even its own library.[22]

The club had reportedly more than 450 boys in 1954.[23] While the Chinese (mostly Teochews) were the majority, there were also Malay, Indian, and Eurasian boys along them. The Boy's Club provided a wide range of activities including badminton, football, basketball, boxing, weight-lifting, chess, and table tennis.

In particular, for table tennis, three tables were provided for the boys to play this popular sport. They became quite good at it: the Boys' Club even won the Tan Thoon Lip Inter-Boys' Club table tennis cup. Robert Yeo, who played the sport using a tennis grip, was Captain one year, with a strong team consisting of a state player,

Tan Hong Meng, Andrew Choo Tien Chye, and Goh Soo Nam, who later went on to play nationally.[24]

By 1958, however, the club started declining, with lack of furniture and insufficient badminton equipment.[25] There were almost no reports of roaring sporting successes from the Boys' Club in the 1960s and 70s. And by 1979, the Upper Serangoon Community Centre moved to new premises in Surin Avenue.[26]

In any case, Robert fortunately found new sporting interests.[27] His old friend who lived in Florence Road, Henry Pang Chan Soon from Serangoon English School, directed his interest towards tennis. Most significantly, Henry was the son of former tennis great, CK Pang, and an excellent tennis player. In fact, CK Pang was former Malayan champion and professional tennis coach (1940s to 1960s), while Henry Pang was former Singapore junior singles champion. From 1962 to 1966, when Robert left for London, he played tennis and effectively stopped playing table tennis.

Tua Jia Kar Village

There was also a Teochew Village where Hougang Street 21 is located. Named after a prominent well in the area, Tua Jia Kar village (or the village at the foot of a big well in Teochew) village was also known as Sompah Serangoon Village.[28]

I had the good fortune to talk to Ng Yew Kang who had memories of Tua Jia Kar village, which he pronounced Tua Che Kar.

Mr Ng said, "I remember that there was a big well at an area called *Tua Che Kar*. There was a row of single-storey brick-structure shops fronting Upper Serangoon Road. Behind the row of shops was a village. There was no tap water in many houses then. The well at the entrance to the village was the main source of drinking water for the villagers. As the well had a rather big diameter and was quite deep, it was referred to as the Big Well. The term *Tua Che Kar* means (the village) near the Big Well.

"As with most residents in Hougang, those living in the village there were mostly Teochews."

By the 1970s, Tua Jia Kar had evolved to become a focal point for gatherings and communal activities for the villagers at Upper Serangoon.[29] It used to be a popular destination for street food, Chinese *wayang* performances, and people listening to yarns spun by storytellers. The well was well-loved and was a source of good and consistent supply of clean water to the villagers, hawkers, and the nearby market. It was so popular among the villagers that they kept drawing from the well even after piped water was later installed at Somapah Serangoon Village.

Memories of Lak Kor Chiok (Sixth Milestone)

*The plaque and replica installed at Hougang Street 21.
Picture taken by the author on 25 August 2019.*

The well was later demolished because of the development of the area, but its legacy remains fondly remembered by the Teochew community living at Upper Serangoon and Hougang.

Today, Kovan City, a bustling centre, stands where the well once stood.[30]

Although the well itself no longer exists, there has been a commemorative plaque and replica installed at Hougang Street 21 since 2005.

The Hougang NPC also wrote a post on Facebook on 30 July 2016 about this ordinary water well which became a landmark, well-remembered by the Teochew community.

Well, when a water well makes it onto social media in the 21st century, one could certainly say that it was popular in the 20th.

Endnotes

1 Robert Yeo, *Routes: A Singaporean Memoir 1940–75*, (Singapore: Ethos Books, 2014), p. 40.

2 Bryan Goh, "Hougang: Diversity in a Teochew Enclave", in *Muse SG*, No. 38, Vol. 11, Issue 02, p. 6.

3 Donald Matheson Dabbs, *The History of Gan Eng Seng School* (Singapore: DM Dabbs, 1992), p. 84.

4 This section is adapted from Serangoon Secondary School, "School History". Source: https://serangoonsec.moe.edu.sg/about-us/school-history. Accessed 3 December 2019. It is also based on Serangoon Secondary School, "SSS Alumni". Source: https://serangoonsec.moe.edu.sg/partnership/sss-alumni. Accessed 3 December 2019.

5 This section is based on the online publication, Singapore Police Force, *Setia Dan Bakti: 50 Stories of Loyalty and Service*, (Singapore: Singapore Police Force, 2015).

6 According to personal communication with Robert Yeo on 1 December 2019.

7 The Straits Times, "Ex-Lib-Soc leader fights 3 newcomers", in *The Straits Times*, 21 May 1959, p. 5.

8 The Singapore Free Press, "Hard work call to colony's leaders", in *The Singapore Free Press*, 3 June 1958, p. 1.

9 Based on a conversation with Robert Yeo on 1 December 2019.

10 Robert Yeo, *op cit.*, pp. 70–72.

11 This section is based on Kirpal Singh, "Meet the Grand Old Man of Singapore Letters…", in *The Straits Times*, 18 May 1980, p. 1.

12 These positions were extracted from a variety of sources. The Straits Times, "Appeal to Local Teachers", in *The Straits Times*, 27 February 1933, p. 6; Malaya Tribune, "Local Teachers' Association", in *Malaya Tribune*, 9 July 1934, p. 18; The Singapore Free Press and Mercantile Advertiser, "Headmaster on Malayan Education", in *The Singapore Free Press and Mercantile Advertiser*, 6 July 1938, p. 7; Malaya Tribune, "Overcrowding In A School", in *Malaya Tribune*, 22 June 1939, p. 7; Malaya Tribune, "Asst. Director of Education", in *Malaya Tribune*, 18 February 1949, p. 2 .

13 The Singapore Free Press and Mercantile Advertiser, "Untitled", in *The Singapore Free Press and Mercantile Advertiser*, 19 August 1939, p. 4.

14 This section is based on The Straits Times, "Spotlight on Malaya and Malayans", in *The Straits Times*, 22 September 1946, p. 2.

15 This section on road names is based on the Montfort-Alumni Singapore's Facebook page. Peter Lim Ah Pin's and Florence Yeo Ah Chee's stories are also based on an oral history interview of James Lim Keng Hoe (born 1916) by Anne Lim Siew Kim (Accession Number 001935, recorded on 12 August 1997).

16 This is based on an oral history interview of James Lim Keng Hoe (born 1916) by Anne Lim Siew Kim, ibid.

17 The Straits Times, "New community centre in S'pore", in *The Straits Times*, 21 April 1953, p. 8.

18 The Straits Times, "Upper Serangoon boys' club formed", in *The Straits Times*, 6 January 1953, p. 7. Also according to personal communication with Robert Yeo on 1 December 2019.

19 According to personal communication with Robert Yeo on 1 December 2019.

20 The Straits Times, "Dramatic club", in *The Straits Times*, 12 August 1957, p. 7.

21 The Singapore Free Press, "This is a Happy Suburb", in *The Singapore Free Press*, 31 May 1954, p. 7.

22 This paragraph is based on The Singapore Free Press, ibid.

23 This paragraph is based on The Singapore Free Press, "Boys Are Proud of Their Club", in *The Singapore Free Press*, 25 June 1954, p. 14.

24 According to personal communication with Robert Yeo on 1 December 2019.

25 Lone Voice, "No furniture, club idle", in *The Straits Times*, 22 March 1958, p. 10.

26 The Straits Times, "CC to shift", in *The Straits Times*, 13 July 1979, p. 13.

27 According to personal communication with Robert Yeo on 1 December 2019.

28 The Straits Times, "The well returns to Tua Jia Ka", in *The Straits Times*, 27 October 1998, p. 31.

29 The rest of this section, unless stated, is based on "Searching for Singapore's Last Water Wells", in *Remember Singapore*. Retrieved from: https://remembersingapore.org/2014/04/19/singapores-last-water-wells/. Updated 2014. Accessed 4 August 2019.

30 Housing & Development Board, "Hougang". Source: http://www.hdb.gov.sg/cs/infoweb/about-us/history/hdb-towns-your-home/hougang. Updated 4 October 2017. Accessed 15 August 2019.

Chapter 7
Memories of Kangkar
(1900s–1986)

Kangkar Fishing Village

Remember Bryan Goh's description of a Teochew Kingdom earlier? The "fishery located at the end of Serangoon Road (around Punggol Park today)" that he was talking about referred to Kangkar fishing village (or simply Kangkar), which referred to a fish market set up in Aukang by Catholic missions in the early 20th century. Kangkar was divided into two by Upper Serangoon Road, and the houses on the north side stood on land belonging to the St Francis Xavier seminary, while those on the south side stood on private land.[1]

In Teochew, "Kang" means river, and "kar" means leg, so Kangkar refers to the "foot of the river". There were other *kangkars* throughout history (with a small "k") in Singapore. After all, as long as there was land at the foot of a river, it would also

The St Francis Xavier Minor Seminary was established in 1925. Those training for the priesthood would spend the first four years here before proceeding to Penang College General for advanced training.

have been called a *kangkar* by Teochews living there. For example, Goh Tong Liang wrote to *The Straits Times* in 1950 to elaborate that Bukit Panjang village, at the 10 ½ mile Bukit Timah Road, was also known as "the Kanka" (without the "r") to residents of all races in that locality, even though there was no river anywhere near.[2]

Basically, an enterprising Teochew pioneer would be in a boat loaded with coolies, food, and tools, along the waters of the *kang*, looking for a suitable place to set up a gambier and pepper plantation. Eventually, his coolies would set up a cluster of shops and houses along a *kangkar*. When they wanted to retrieve supplies or food, they would refer to the place as *kangkar*.

However, when new batches of coolies arrived, some would hear this term and refer to any cluster of shops and houses as a *kangkar*, that is why the word eventually lost its original association with rivers and came to mean a cluster of shops and houses anywhere.

An artist's impression of the fishing village of Kangkar shows energy and bustling activity.

In this case, this was *a* real kangkar; or some would say, *the* real kangkar. Kangkar Fishing Village was a fishing port with a fishing village situated at the end of Upper Serangoon. The Kangkar fish merchants set up office in attap huts clustered around the wholesale market, which was just a roof held up by wooden posts, set on the pier.[3]

Most of Kangkar's villagers made their living by fishing near Horsburgh Lighthouse.[4] In June 1983, *The Straits Times* reported that Kangkar was a home base for about 90 offshore fishing boats and 16 fish merchants, with 40 tonnes of fish changing hands in a few hours each morning.[5] The same report stated that in 1982, its merchants handled 13,607 tonnes of fish, an increase of 18.6 percent over 1981. For comparison, while these numbers were respectable, they were not as huge as the numbers coming from Jurong. There, the 92 merchants at Jurong's more famous fishing port and Central Fish Market auctioned 150 to 200 tonnes of fish each morning, brought in by foreign and local fishing vessels at night.

Many of the fishermen and merchants lived in the area. For example, fish merchant, Lim Boon Chek, who ran a company called Seng Long Soon Kee with 4 other partners and employed 20 workers and clerks who all lived at Kangkar, was born and bred at Kangkar.[6]

The Straits Times described the way the Kangkar market operated:[7]

> The Kangkar wholesale fish market operates as a very loose form of auction. Sellers call out prices of items that are not moving, then nimbly run them up or down from moment to moment, following the trend of demand.
>
> If two buyers want a particular tray of goods, they have to outbid each other.
>
> Some hang around for hours, waiting for the price of slower moving items to hit rock bottom before buying.
>
> The merchants work out transactions on calculator or abacus and record sales (which peter off at around 8 a.m.) in hardbound exercise books.
>
> They collect the cash—or even give credit to trusted hawkers—and distribute it later to the various fishermen, after deducting six to eight per cent commission.
>
> Outsiders get snubbed, for they tend to misread the delicate bargaining signals or do not understand the lingua franca, which is predominantly Teochew.

Kangkar Through the Eyes of Mr Lee Boon Kee

Born in 1943, Boon Kee is a retired primary school principal. His family moved to Kangkar when he was four years old. Below are his reminiscences of his childhood experiences, from a written account shared with my father as his friend and schoolmate.

> I was four years old when my family moved from Chinatown to Kangkar village. Kangkar consisted of about 150 households and most of them lived in wooden houses with attap roofs. There were only three double-storey brick houses. One of them was occupied by the government maternity clinic where some nurses lived. The second was a huge mansion with acres of garden and the last one was where my family lived.
>
> We did not occupy the whole building, but only the rear ground floor apartment. It consisted of one bedroom, a sitting room and an annex used as a kitchen. Two other families lived upstairs. The front was the landlord's provision shop.
>
> Some of the kids in the kampung did not attend school. They played and roamed about the whole day long. I thought I was unfortunate having to attend Holy Innocents' English School, as Montfort School was then called.
>
> Upper Serangoon Road ran right through the middle of Kangkar with most of the houses clustered on either side. The road ended at the jetty which jutted into the river. Every year while I was living there, there would be an occasion or two when a drunken driver would plunge his car into the river. The commotion would wake up everybody in the kampung and soon the jetty would be crowded with curious onlookers. I was too young to know whether anyone died in the accident. The unfortunate driver and his passengers would be fished out of the river and sent to the hospital.
>
> I remember a particular evening when there was a big commotion in Kangkar. News spread that a huge crocodile was brought in by a boat. So we all ran to the jetty to view it. True enough, there was a huge crocodile, all wrapped up in fishing nets. It was said to weigh at least 300 kilograms and took eight muscular men to haul it up

from the boat to the jetty and then to carry it to the auction shed. As a kid, I wondered who would want to buy a monster like that.

From between 4 pm and 7 pm motorized boats would start coming into Kangkar, bringing their catch from the *kelongs* in the north eastern coast of Singapore. Some *kelongs* were also from the seas off the south eastern coast of Johore. The boats would be tied up at the jetty and started off-loading their catch. Workers, many of them my neighbours, would haul the huge crates to the giant shed, a short distance from the jetty. Here, other workers would sort out the fish, cover them with ice and arrange them in neat piles on the floor ready for the buyers.

Early the next morning the shed would be a busy hive of activities. Buyers in all kinds of contraptions, some on motorcycles with an attached side-car, would buy the catch for resale to consumers. If I went to the shed early, I would be able to see my next-door neighbour who was a widow with two children buying the cheapest types of fish and other seafood, putting them in her two carry baskets. She would carry them and walk to several kampungs to sell the fish. This was how she made a living and supported two children. Her children, however, did not attend school.

The big mansion which was about half a kilometer from my house was a great mystery. It was called Meng Chiang Hng and reputed to be haunted. Nobody could tell for sure what that really meant. However we kampung folks could see families moving in with all their household items like furniture and pots and pans one day and then a week or two later moving out hurriedly. As kids we were afraid of the house, but we were not afraid of the garden. We steered clear of the house but we would sneak into the garden regularly. The red luscious rambutan, *jambu* or *chiku* fruits proved too tempting. And in the day time the ghost would be more afraid of us. Families kept on moving in and out in quick succession. From my own observation, no family over stayed for more than two months. The house exuded an eerie feeling. At night when people had to pass by the house, they crossed the road and walked on the opposite side.

My house was beside Upper Serangoon Road. The back faced

a vacant plot of land about the size of a football field. At the far end stood a tiny hut and there after the ground sloped down and the big swampy area started. At low tide the black mud was exposed for a considerable area before the mangrove forest took over. This muddy area was my playground. At low tide, you could wade into the mud often sinking in up to your knees. I had learned from my neighbor, Boon Teck, the widow's son, how to catch razor clam. He taught me how to use a slab of bamboo, look for a distinct shaped hole in the mud and dig the bamboo in and then lever it up. Lo and behold! The mud would open up and in the midst you would find a razor clam.

I would catch half a bucket of razor clams in a couple of hours. In America, digging razor clams is a New Year's tradition for many families but when I did this I, a child, was putting food on the table for my family. I also helped in another way: I wandered about the neighbourhood looking for wood so that my mother would not have to spend money buying charcoal and firewood for cooking. I ended up collecting mainly wood bark in the river, a very good source of fuel when dried in the sun.

During high tide, there would be puddles of sea water here and there on the mud. The water would be crystal clear unless you disturbed the mud. You could see small prawns, small fish and quite often sea snakes trapped in the pool when the tide receded. It was a sport and a challenge for us to catch the snake without being bitten. The trick was to dip into the water, grab the snake by the tail and hold it up away from your body. Then by swinging it, like you would swing a rope, the poor creature would be groggy and be in no position to bite you! But you would be kind and let it go.

Kangkar Through the Eyes of Mr Ng Kok Song

In 2012, Ng Kok Song (then 64 years old), a former Government of Singapore Investment Corporation (GIC) Chief Investment Officer, shared with *The Straits Times* about his fishing village roots, where Sengkang East is located today, near the tail end of Upper Serangoon Road. From the time he was born until he was married at 24 in 1972, he lived in a house with a thatched roof, mud floor, and two bedrooms in Kangkar. He was the second of 11 children, and his father was a fish auctioneer at the fish market while his mother was a housewife.

Ng Kok Song shared about the touching memories of his life in the fishing village with a busy fish market peopled by Teochews and Catholics living in farms and attap houses. According to an interview with *The Straits Times*:

> Baptised a Catholic when he was seven years old, he was up before the crack of dawn each morning to serve as an altar boy at the nearby Church of the Nativity of the Blessed Virgin Mary... After classes at nearby Montfort School, where he studied for 12 years, he had to look after his younger siblings.
>
> 'When I came home from school, I would put them into sarong hammocks and rock them to sleep. In the evenings, I took them out for a walk,' he says.
>
> In between, he had to feed the family's 80 chickens, collect the eggs and clean out the coops. The birds were sold during festive periods such as Chinese New Year to help supplement the family income.
>
> Thanks to his father's job, they always had fish for lunch and dinner but life was far from easy.
>
> 'One of the things which made me sad was my mother having to borrow money from neighbours when things got desperate,' he says.
>
> Fortunately, they had helpful neighbours and a kind granduncle.[8]

At the time, Kangkar had gangsters and teenagers often belonged to gangs and participated in street clashes, but Ng Kok Song credited the positive influence of the Catholic Church and the Gabrielite Brothers for keeping him on the straight and narrow path.

> 'Kangkar was infested with gangsters. There were always clashes on the streets and many teenagers belonged to gangs,' he recalls.
>
> 'But I fell under the influence of the church and the Gabrielite Brothers.'...
>
> Mr Ng, who was his school's head prefect, contemplated becoming a priest in his early teens. After his A levels, he won a scholarship to study engineering in Canada but around that time, his father lost his voice and that cost him his job.

> 'Dad couldn't bear to tell me, so he got one of my good friends to speak to me. He said the family could not afford to let me go abroad or to go to university and that I had to start working to support the family.
>
> 'I told my dad I would support the family by giving private tuition but I had to go to university.'
>
> He kept his word. He won himself a Public Service Commission scholarship to study physics at the University of Singapore, and gave private tuition to half a dozen students. The few hundred dollars he earned each month were handed over to the family...
>
> He is happy with how life has turned out. His siblings have done well and work in different professions—from finance to engineering. They have given him more than 20 nephews and nieces. Most of them, as well as his 88-year-old mother, live in Hougang, a stone's throw from Kangkar.[9]

Other Memories of Kangkar

Other memories of Kangkar included Mdm Chong Ah Yong's story, from Serene Ng's interview with her for the Singapore Memory Project.[10] Mdm Chong (born 1947) came to Singapore from Malaysia in 1965, when Singapore became independent. She first lived with her in-laws in Punggol. In 1973, she moved into her own home in nearby Kangkar.

Mdm Chong's husband was a fisherman. He would go on his offshore fishing trips on board the fishing vessel, SMF 740, with each trip lasting about four days and three nights. Naturally, she was worried for his safety. In his later years, he stopped going out to sea and sold fish at the Kangkar fish market until his death at age 57.

Mdm Chong remembers with fondness the years in Kangkar, living in an attap house surrounded by family and friends. As the kampung was near the sea, there were occasional floods. Despite that, life was good. She had no worries and she enjoyed the carefree natural environment. There was no need to lock your door and small animals roamed freely.

However, Kangkar sat on land which was needed for road and new town development, and its river silted up too heavily at low tide.[11] Boats could not come in during low tide because of its shallow water and had to wait for high tide to unload their catch and take up bunkering.[12] In addition, the village developed on its own with no proper planning as fishermen built the facilities as and when they were needed. As a result, the small fish market was by the 1980s old, congested, and crowded.

In 1984, the Kangkar fish merchants moved to a new wholesale complex at Punggol, while the last of the few hundred villagers were resettled in 1986.[13] The government acquired the land around the Kangkar fish centre for Hougang New Town and the extension of Upper Serangoon Road.[14] Kangkar Community Centre at Upper Serangoon Road, which was formerly called Punggol Community Centre, was closed at the end of October 1984—unfortunately only bearing the name Kangkar for five years.[15]

Augustine Low, writing for *The Straits Times*, reported in 1986 that his childhood village of Kangkar was deserted, awaiting redevelopment.

> When I visited it last week, I saw not a speck of life—only torn-down houses, muddy footpaths and the old fish market on the pier still held up by wooden posts were all that remained…
>
> It was said that anyone born and bred in Kangkar could do two things—tell the freshness of fish by just one look, and speak Teochew.
>
> And because more than 90 per cent of Kangkar villagers were Teochews, the dialect was the lingua franca and even the handful of Malays and Eurasians could speak it…
>
> Bedtime came early for many villagers, especially those who had to be up at 4 am to go to the wholesale fish market.
>
> But for a whole week every year, during the Seventh Moon Festival, Teochew operas played all-night long to appreciative villagers at an open ground.
>
> For the children, it was an occasion to revel in the carnival-like atmosphere, with itinerant hawkers plying an endless variety of trades and sweetmeats.
>
> The occasional appearance by the comedian duo of Wang Sa and Ya Fong would be greeted with delirious cheers, their jokes in Teochew always striking a chord with the audience.[16]

Teochew John Liow Boon Peng, a former Kangkar resident who was born at home in Lorong Santun in 1969, was one of those who watched the opera with his brothers when he was a young boy growing up in the 1970s. Both his father and mother and their families were Catholic Teochews. He recalled old times at Kangkar fondly:

> In the lunar seventh month, there would be the *Gor Tai* (getai) held at an empty space on the other side of the road near to the Kangkar harbour. I remember my brothers and I would go and watch these *Gor Tais* but I never really took a liking to them, but only to the street food such as *yang-or jui* (bird's nest drink) or *putu piring* from the itinerant hawkers. As we were really poor, we could only afford very few of these luxuries, and could only afford them once or twice throughout the seventh month using our limited pocket money.
>
> I recall there was a small stream which ran from the side of one of the lanes which Lorong Santun split into as one walked deeper in from the Upper Serangoon end, before Lorong Santun joined Punggol Road on the other side (where Punggol Park is now). I used to catch guppies from the stream or followed that lane deeper into the *payoh* (swamp). There, besides guppies, we could catch *bua kee* (swamp or mangrove crabs) or *long gao her* (drain guppies) and dig for clams. To catch *bua kee*, we would use a stick with the piece of string from a drinks plastic bag tied with a moving knot to hook a claw of the *bua kee*. We would bring home the larger crabs for my mum to clean and marinate with soya sauce and chilli. The marinated *bua kee* really went well with porridge…
>
> Today, the area has changed tremendously and it's no longer as rustic as before. I miss the fishing boats and harbour at Kangkar.[17]

Even when it was gone, Kangkar village still retained a strong pull for its former residents and many had fond memories of the area.

In 1986, Kangkar was a shell of what it was formerly, but Mr Loh Kiam Chung shared with *The Straits Times* that he and other former neighbours—fish and ice dealers among them—still went back every morning to their old house in Kangkar village.[18] A wooden home built in the 1930s, home to three families who stayed there till 1984, and falling apart at the time, served as an informal "clubhouse" to Mr Loh and his family and friends, who still went back for breakfast and cooked their meals just as they used to before.

Even though the Kangkar wholesale market and its traders had made way for progress in the form of the $11 million Punggol Fishing Port and Wholesale Fish Market five kilometres down the road, it still retained strong sentimental value for the former residents. They planned to keep something of the old days alive—while everything of value had been taken to their new Hougang homes, they still kept the three-walled kitchen of their old home stocked with what was needed to boil porridge and a kettle of coffee.

Women in their 60s and 70s walked from their new homes in Hougang to buy from the hawker at Kangkar because, as one of them said, the fish in other places will not be as fresh as the ones they can get at Kangkar.

Even the boatbuilder Mr Koh Ah Tee travelled from his home in Havelock Road to Kangkar six days a week, to look after his boat and… just in case a buyer came along.

Remember Mdm Chong Ah Yong, whose story we shared earlier? Like many, she lived in Kangkar until the area was slated for redevelopment in the 1980s.[19] Despite redevelopment, she did not leave Hougang. In fact, in 1984, she moved into a flat at Hougang St 11. Moving to a flat was a lifestyle change, but she adapted to it. The flat was larger and cleaner, but she missed her old home and especially her friends.

Over the years, her new neighbours also moved away and other families moved in. These days, she keeps her door closed most times. She passes her time helping at her son-in-law's hairdressing salon nearby. She goes on trips with some of her neighbours and also spends time at the community centre nearby, participating in activities there. She enjoys eating the *wonton mee* and *nasi lemak* at the nearby Lorong Ah Soo market. For shopping, she and her neighbours frequent the nearby shopping centres at Serangoon and Kovan.

Kangkar Mall at Hougang.

Some pictures from the wall at Kangkar food court at Kangkar Mall.

At Hougang today, there stands a mall called Kangkar Mall, with a heritage wall which shares the apocryphal story of a fisherman who became a hero.

Part of Sengkang was eventually built over the area which Kangkar once occupied. Sengkang, or "prosperous harbour" in Chinese, derives its name from a road called Lorong Sengkang, off Lorong Buangkok. Nevertheless, Kangkar's history and heritage is still retained in the town's design, with the theme, "Town of the Seafarer". And to top it all, there is a Light Rail Transit (LRT) station called Kangkar in Sengkang. At least its memory has been retained.

Kangkar Light Rail Transit in Sengkang.

It is a pity that Kangkar had to go because of development. But as the Latin saying goes:

> *Tempora mutantur, nos et mutamur in illis.*

Or, in English:

> *Times change, and we change with the times.*

But there was one place which—seemingly—did not change with the times, which someone termed "Paradise Preserved".

The Last Kampung in Singapore—Kampong Lorong Buangkok

A sign indicating mainland Singapore's last kampung. This photograph was taken by the author on 23 December 2018.

In the mid-1970s, my father moved to a brick house near Kampung Lorong Buangkok. When I found out about this fact, I excitedly asked my father, "Did you actually live near mainland Singapore's last kampung?"

"Yes," he said. "I lived at 369 Lorong Buangkok. The house was rented from my friend's brother, for $700. You know, I can still remember the house number till this day simply because of its uniqueness, as we used to refer to dogs as *sa luck* (three six in Teochew)."

But unfortunately, my father did not stay there long as he moved out of Aukang in 1975.

This is the story of Lorong Buangkok.[20] According to Eisen Teo, Lorong Buangkok actually ran across much of what is Sengkang today, connecting Yio Chu Kang Road to Punggol Road.[21] "Buangkok" was the Teochew name for Bukit Sembawang Rubber Company, which owned land in the area. In the late 1970s, nine tracks were carved out from Lorong Buangkok and expunged for Sengkang New Town.

Then-Managing Director of Lycos Asia Shobha Tsering Bhalla wrote an amazing piece called "Paradise Preserved" for *Today* in 2002, and detailed the idyllic rural habitat of the three-acre little kampung of 30 houses with close-knit neighbours:[22]

> …Just as the old-fashioned architecture of the kampung reflects the traditional spirit of sharing, trust and kinship of the community that lives in it, its denizens serve as a living reminder of the common racially-neutral heritage that all Singaporeans share.
>
> For, long before the high-rises and regimented housing divided the island into "tongues and tax brackets", it was the generous spirit of the kampung that dominated our lives, regardless of whether we were Malay, Chinese, Indians, Eurasians or Others…
>
> Ask Mr Jamil how many times his Chinese neighbours have repaired and re-roofed his house, free of charge.
>
> Or listen to 33-year-old driving instructor Mohd Zulkifli tell you how Ms Sng Mui Hong, the village "headman", checks in on his 60-year-old mother and 70-year-old step-father almost daily when she passes by on her way home…

Shobha Tsering Bhalla also reflected on the kampung spirit, linking it with the Singapore Spirit.

> Therefore, all the more reason that it should cling to this little village off Ang Mo Kio as the last vestige of a time when the Kampung Spirit was synonymous with the Singapore Spirit—with this little island's

sense of nationhood.

This spirit is best exemplified by 48-year-old Ms Sng. Her father, who was a herbalist, bought the plot of land in 1956 and leased it out. In all these years, the rent has hardly ever risen.

Most tenants pay about $15 a month and Ms Sng herself lives simply, tending to most menial tasks like cleaning the public drains herself. But what grabs the imagination is Ms Sng herself.

The touching sense of social responsibility and lack of greed that is evident in this amazing woman's refusal to raise rentals or cave in to the attractive offerings of developers is something that should be held up and admired at a time when the "economy" has become the new arbiter of morality.

Well said; I agree.

Endnotes

1. John Clammer, *The Sociology of Singapore Religion: Studies in Christianity and Chinese Culture* (Singapore: Chopmen Publishers, 1991), p. 71.

2. The Straits Times, "On The Margin", in *The Straits Times*, 5 April 1950, p.6.

3. The Straits Times, "Auctioning will go on at new site", in *The Straits Times*, 17 June 1983, p. 4.

4. K. K. Fong, "The end of 'Kangkar' village?", in *New Nation*, 28 April 1977, p. 2.

5. The Straits Times, "Auctioning will go on at new site", *op cit.*

6. Ibid.

7. This section was based on The Straits Times, "Auctioning will go on at new site", *op cit.*

8. Ng Kok Song, cited in Wong Kim Hoh, "GIC Chief's Unlikely Fishing Village Roots", in *The Straits Times*, 8 April 2012, p. 33.

9. Ibid.

10. This section is based on Serene Ng's interview with Mdm Chong Ah Yong.

11. The Straits Times, "Farewell Kangkar", in *The Straits Times*, 17 June 1983, p. 2.

12. The Straits Times, "Auctioning will go on at new site", *op cit.*

13. Augustine Low, "Kangkar, once noted for fresh fish and Teochews", in *The Straits Times*, 30 September 1986, p. 16.

14. The Straits Times, "Auctioning will go on at new site", *op cit.*

15. This finding is based on The Straits Times, "Kangka CC", in *The Straits Times*, 27 August 1979, p. 8 and The Straits Times, "Closing date", in *The Straits Times*, 3 October 1984, p. 16.

16. Augustine Low, *op cit.*

17. Personal communication with John Liow on 11 December 2019.

18. This section is based on Audrey Perera, "Kangkar village draws fond ex-residents back", in *The Straits Times*, 21 December 1986, p. 22.

19. This section is based on Serene Ng's interview with Mdm Chong Ah Yong.

20. In Eugene Wijeysingha's book, *Down the Seletar River: Discovering a Hidden Treasure of Singapore*, Lorong Buangkok is part of Seletar. According to the book, Seletar includes Jalan Kayu, Seletar Airbase, and parts of Ang Mo Kio, Yio Chu Kang, and Lorong Buangkok.

21. This paragraph is based on Eisen Teo, *Jalan Singapura: 700 Years of Movement in Singapore* (Singapore: Marshall Cavendish, 2020), p. 233.

22. The next few sections are based on Shobha Tsering Bhalla, "Paradise preserved", in *Today*, 18 April 2002, p. 37.

Chapter 8
Memories of Punggol

Remember how the term Punggol could refer to either Aukang or Punggol proper? This chapter is about Punggol proper.

According to Michelle Chan, Punggol today refers to the area bounded by Tampines Expressway, Sungei Serangoon, and Sungei Punggol.[1] It consists of 11 districts, 7 of which—Waterway East, Waterway West, Northshore, Matilda, Punggol Point, Canal, and Crescent— are waterfront housing districts.[2]

Somewhat similar to what my father said, Michelle Chan pointed out that from the colonial era up to the 1970s, what was considered Punggol included Sengkang and Buangkok, which, as my father explained to me, were considered part of Aukang. She argued that this large historical boundary explained why Punggol possessed both coastal and agricultural characteristics.

An artist's impression of the houses at Punggol, near the beach.

The first use of the name "Pongul", which eventually evolved into "Punggol", was by John Turnbull Thomson in his 1844 land survey map. There are several possible explanations for the name "Punggol", all sharing Malay origins. First, the name could refer to the practice of hurling sticks at the branches of fruit trees to bring the fruits down to the ground, or it can refer to a place where fruits and forest produce are offered for wholesale, implying that Punggol was a rural, agricultural area. Another explanation of the name's origin comes from Awang bin Osman, whom you read about earlier in this book.

This makes for an interesting anecdote. In an interview with the National Archives of Singapore, Awang bin Osman claimed that Wak Sumang, his great grandfather, gave Punggol its name. The story goes that Wak Sumang had obtained approval from the British to start a new village. While he was clearing his garden, a large tree was burnt, and its branch—known as *punggur* in Malay—fell onto his hut. As a result, he decided to name the village punggur, which later evolved into Punggol.

Regardless, these different interpretations of how Punggol came to be named all had the common theme that its name was related to its rural location and bucolic landscape.

On 1 September 2019, HDB announced that two new Punggol Build-To-Order (BTO) housing estates with a total of 2,724 flats within Punggol Point Crown and Punggol Point Cove would pay tribute to Punggol's history and heritage.[3] The projects capitalised on Punggol's history, with heritage elements in their designs which help residents appreciate their town's roots.

For example, Punggol Point Crown, inspired by the old Punggol Zoo, was planned along five thematic zones based on natural habitats such as the forest, grassland, and shoreline. It was reported that a special heritage walk—a first in new BTO projects—inspired by the zoo would weave through the precinct.

And Punggol Point Cove, located along the eastern shoreline of Punggol Point, was reportedly inspired by Punggol's past as a fishing village, drawing reference from Punggol's humble beginnings as a fishing village, and later as a fishing port.

Memories of Punggol from the Eyes of Ng Yew Kang

Speaking with Mr Ng Yew Kang, I learnt about his interesting memories of Punggol. He began sharing more about Kangkar first, and said, "The Kangkar fisheries port at the end of Upper Serangoon Road was shifted to a port further down in Punggol Road.

"The daily catch of fisheries which landed in Kangkar port were sold in the nearby Lim Tua Tow and Simon Road Markets. They were noted for their freshness as the time from landing to market was only about half an hour. However, when the Punggol Fishery Port later moved to Jurong, the fish sold in the Lim Tua Tow and Simon Road Markets were not as fresh as before, because of the much greater time lapse from landing to these two markets."

Taking a deep breath, he said, "In fact, the whole of Kangkar and Punggol have transformed beyond recognition. My brothers, friends, and I used to cycle all the way from Surin Lane to a seaside spot at the end of Punggol 17th Avenue to swim. The site was known as *Seng Hu Ti* (Priest's Land) as it was near a bungalow belonging to the Catholic church. It was a popular swimming spot with the youth then.

"There used to be two popular restaurants on both sides at the end of Punggol Road where the bus terminus was. Many people from all over Singapore went there for seafood and local food such as Chinese style *mee goreng*, which they were known for."

Suddenly, he said, "In the sea a short distance from Punggol Point, there was also a big floating restaurant serving seafood and Chinese cuisine. It was a huge *kelong*-like structure a short sampan ride from Punggol Point.

"The only one of its kind in Singapore then, it was very popular with the connoisseurs from all over Singapore. It was visible from the shore and was brightly lit at night, giving a spectacular sight. I understand it was modelled after the Jumbo Floating Restaurant in Hong Kong."

My father also told me, "The floating restaurant was known as Sea Palace. During those days, it was really unique to have a restaurant in the sea. It was quite an experience as you had to go there by boat. You had to climb up as if you were going to a *kelong*. That was quite an experience. In those days, there were not many ways to entertain oneself, not like today. I spent a lot of money there. Once, I tipped a waitress $1.50 which was a lot of money in those days!"

However, sometimes nice places face tragic ends.

Mr Ng said, "Unfortunately, it was destroyed by a fire not long after it was open for business."

The "Haunted House"—Punggol's Matilda House

"For your book, you should also write about the haunted Matilda House," said my father. "Go find out about it."

I groaned, "Haunted house? I'm a man of science... well, social science."

But being a dutiful son, I followed up on this ghostly lead and did some research.

Luckily for me, some houses contain such extraordinary stories within their walls that they get talked about even after their occupants have moved out. This "haunted house" was one such example.

Located off Punggol Road, the Matilda House goes by many names, such as *Istana Menanti* ("Waiting Palace" in Malay) or the Punggol Kampong House.[4] The house was originally constructed in 1902 by Alexander Cashin, as a gift for his wife. It was named Matilda in honour of Alexander's mother, according to Howard Cashin (1920–2009), Alexander's son.

The Cashin's family history in Singapore can be traced back to the early 1840s. As they were a prominent family, Cashin Street, off North Bridge Road, was named after them.

Alexander's father Joseph William Cashin was a lawyer's clerk who eventually became the first Eurasian millionaire in Singapore. The secret to his fortune was money from opium farms, which were legal in the 1880s, and subsequently real estate. The Cashin family owned a vast quantity of land and properties, including the conserved house at 23 Amber Road.

The wealthy family considered Matilda House a weekend resort.[5] It had a statement red roof that could be seen from afar along with white walls and two large staircases. Well-manicured lawns and tropical flowers were lined up at the frontage, showing the wealth of the family. It had open verandas and raised floors which boasted great ventilation and style. The single-story building spread across 417 square metres and had a total of six bedrooms. It even had a servants' quarters attached to it. In its prime, Matilda House also had a fully functional stable, an orchard, and a tennis court. The orchard had mangosteen, durian, and rambutan trees.

There are many quirky anecdotes starring the Cashin family and the Matilda House. When it was first built, there was a path leading to the Punggol River with an unobstructed view of the Straits of Johor. Anecdotally, the Sultan of Johor would visit the Cashins by boat for a cup of tea.

Besides visits by the Sultan, the house saw many other exciting events, including helicopter landings. In 1989, the *New Paper* reported the impending exciting landing of two helicopters on the garden lawns of Matilda House:

> **TWO helicopters will descend on the green lawns of Matilda House in Punggol on Sunday.**
> **The landings have to do with a party to be held by the Singapore**

Memories of Punggol

> Chapter of the American Helicopter Society. The owners of the house had given the society permission to hold its family day on the spacious lawns.[6]

However, helicopter landings on its grounds were only a minor footnote in Matilda House's long history—it also saw many other exciting events. The house was used for the filming of two TV series, the BBC's Tenko and Grundy Television's Tanamera. It even survived a Japanese takeover during the Second World War: the Japanese Navy took over Matilda House in 1942. Later, when the war ended, the British Royal Navy occupied it, and the Cashins only got back the house in 1946.

In the 1950s, Punggol comprised mainly pig and poultry farms and rubber or coconut plantations. All of these eventually made way for high-rise HDB apartments, to convert the area into a residential new town.

Following this, Matilda House was set to be demolished.

However, this demolishment did not go as planned, because the Matilda House soon earned a reputation for being haunted.

Remember, my father did tell me something to that effect, but being a man of (social) science, I did not take what he said seriously.

That is, until, I read an article on Goody Feed (a website).

According to the Goody Feed Team, three of the workers who were supposed to help in the demolition of the house died of unnatural causes, causing the demolition project to be abandoned, and leading outsiders to believe that there was an entity inside the house.[7] This entity was hostile towards anyone who tried to enter the house. It was not long before reports of a pale woman wearing a white dress started floating around. Some people who got a glimpsing view described her as a full body apparition that floated around like mist. Some accounts say that they spotted a lady with long hair sitting on the branches of surrounding trees as well. Another writer actually explored the place, and commented that the estate was damp and dirty, but that was not what caught his attention. He could hear noises when he was looking through a room, and when he was exiting the house he could swear someone forcibly pushed him out.

For whatever reason, supernatural or not, the house was left abandoned for over two decades.[8] The house was gazetted on 21 February 2000 for conservation, according to the Urban Redevelopment Authority.[9]

Jose Raymond wrote about the dilapidated kampung house in Punggol standing amidst development:[10]

> "Every piece of land in Punggol has been levelled but the house is still standing." said a resident, Mrs Lee Heng Siok. Mdm Perumal Arokiasamy, 66, said the view of Istana Menanti from her flat was "so scary that it sent shivers down her spine" even when she stared at the house in broad daylight...
>
> So, TODAY turned to Urban Redevelopment Authority (URA) to shed some light on the "mystery".
>
> Istana Menanti—whose real name is Matilda House—has not been torn down because "it has been gazetted for conservation", said URA spokeswoman Serene Tng.
>
> The house was built in 1902 by Mr Joseph Cashin, whose family history in Singapore can be traced back to the 1840s.
>
> The house—an example of an early style tropical bungalow—was put on the conservation list in 2000.
>
> "It is the only remaining bungalow in Punggol," Ms Tng said.
>
> Still, if it is deemed worthy to be put on the list, why does it look so run down?
>
> She said that by gazetting the building, URA had taken the "first step to have it remain untouched and there will be plans to have it conserved".

The house was eventually slated to be restored for use as a clubhouse for the residents of A Treasure Trove, a new condominium that was being constructed.[11] In December 2010, property developer Sim Lian Group acquired the site when it was put up for sale; the sale conditions included the need to retain and restore Matilda House according to conservation guidelines, and integrate it as part of the housing project. It eventually became a clubhouse for residents of A Treasure Trove condominium.

Many historians and history enthusiasts were glad to see the Matilda House being integrated into the new building rather than being demolished. The conditions for turning the house into a clubhouse ensured that the house was properly renovated after years of disrepair. However, it managed to retain its charm and style by becoming part of the condominium.

Well, in an ideal world, the Matilda House would exist on its own without being changed or demolished.

But change is the price we pay for urbanisation and development.

Endnotes

1. This section, unless otherwise stated, is drawn from material by Michelle Chan Yun Yee, "Punggol: Waves of Recreation", in *MuseSG*, Vol. 11, Issue 1–2018.
2. As reported in Channel NewsAsia, "HDB to launch BTO projects in Punggol inspired by early zoo, fishing village", in *Channel NewsAsia*, 1 September 2019.
3. Ibid.
4. This paragraph is based on the Urban Redevelopment Authority web article, "Matilda House". Source: https://www.ura.gov.sg/Conservation-Portal/Explore/History?bldgid=PGLRD. Updated 2019. Accessed 17 July 2019.
5. This section is also based on Daniel Ng, "Matilda House". Source: https://stateofbuildings.sg/places/matilda-house. Updated 2015. Accessed 17 July 2019.
6. This section is based on Loh Tuan Lee, "Matilda House and memories", in *New Paper*, 28 August 1989, p. 4.
7. These rumours are from the Goody Feed Team, "The story behind the haunted Matilda House in Punggol". Source: https://goodyfeed.com/the-story-behind-the-haunted-matilda-house-in-punggol/. Updated 2019. Accessed 17 July 2019.
8. This section is also based on Daniel Ng, *op cit*.
9. Urban Redevelopment Authority, *op cit*.
10. Jose Raymond, "Mystery behind the last 'palace' standing in Punggol", in *Today*, 3 September 2002, p. 1.
11. This section is based on Lim Yi Han, "Matilda House gets new life as condo clubhouse", in *The Straits Times*, 18 October 2012, and Rachel Tan, "Matilda, a grand old house in Punggol", in *The Sunday Times*, 2 September 2013.

Chapter 9
Kampung Memories (1946–1975)

My father shared his memories of the kampung with me, from houses to food, entertainment, and many other aspects of everyday life. And these stories helped me understand him much better.

Everyday Life: Houses

First, I start with every Singaporean's favourite topic: the property market. I enjoy a good conversation about properties every now and then. My father is no exception. He told me about his categorisation of different types of housing options available in Aukang then, but they were probably common across Singapore.

My father said, "The first and most basic type of housing was the *Ah Tup chu*, or attap house, which had roofs with nipah leaves, which had to be fully or partially replaced every few years before wear and tear. From 1946 to 1953, we lived at Lorong Low Koon, which was my grandmother's land, and then moved to a house in Jalan Payoh Lai, rented for $20 a month. These houses were *Ah Tup chu*.

"A slight improvement was *Sar Lee chu*—houses with zinc roofs and wooden walls. You'd know when it rained, because it was so noisy! We lived in Jalan Lye Kwee from 1957 onwards. More memorably one side of the house was made of wood, and one time, when the wood rotted and left a gap, we patched it with paper and painted the white paper blue, to match the walls. We rented this for $50 a month at first, before it was raised to $55.

"In those days, the best type of house was called *Ang Mo chu* or western house–these were brick houses with roof tiles, and the best and most expensive. When we stayed at Lorong Buangkok in the mid-1970s, we stayed in an *Ang Mo chu*, rented for $700 a month!

My father (right) and his neighbour, outside the Sar Lee chu at Jalan Lye Kwee. Picture was taken circa 1970.

"The flooring of houses often comprised cement, and in the very poor attap houses it was even possible to have clay flooring, with the clay levelled out.

"Most houses were standalone, or bungalows. Most were single-storey, except for some *Ang Mo chu*. Those were the types of houses we lived in during those times."

Kampung house at Jalan Hock Chye, Aukang, where Edmund Arozoo lived from 1947 to 1977. Photo by the late Harold Arozoo; courtesy of Edmund M Arozoo.

An unusual house in Aukang with a roof made of both attap and zinc. Picture was taken in the 1980s. Courtesy of S. Lim.

Kampung Memories (1946–1975)

Juliana Teo, writing about her memories of Holy Innocents' Lane in 1972, shared the following story about the home she grew up in:

> I grew up in 50A Holy Innocents Lane. We lived in a big house which had 6 bedrooms with my father, mother and his siblings and mother. The house was rectangle in shape, unpainted with a thatched roof made of coconut leaves[1] [sic]. There was a verandah [sic] with 2 long rectangle chairs which could seat 6 persons each. The kitchen was huge—and my mother was allowed to partition half of the kitchen to cook for us in the 70s. The huge compound in front of the house had a water well, some fruit trees and a bank of the Punggol River. As a child, I grew up swimming in the swamp sometimes, avoiding huge snakes which swam with us. Our relatives all stayed around us in the compound—my uncles set up their own homes within feet of the mother house. It wasn't always happy though—squabbles and jealousies were common especially among the adults when the children got into scuffles…
>
> Now Holy Innocents' Lane has disappeared due to development. It is probably Hougang Ave 10 and filled with flats. You would not be able to locate the exact spot where my house was situated.[2]

She was not the only one who lived in a big house. Ng Yew Kang, sharing about his childhood home with me, said, "When I was young, I lived in a two-storey detached house made of timber, with a roof made of small triangular tiles at 14 Surin Lane. It had an area of approximately 7,000 square feet."

"Was it expensive to stay there?" I asked.

Mr Ng replied, "It was large; yet, it was affordable. At the time, we rented this house for approximately $10 per month. The rent remained cheap even long after the Japanese Occupation ended because of rent control by the British colonial government; during my family's stay there, the rent for the house was $40 or $50 per month at the most."

(The topic of rent control keeping houses affordable was interesting to me, so I looked it up later. As it turns out, the British introduced rent control in 1947 to restrict a landlord's right to increase the rent of, or remove the tenant from, a rent-controlled property.[3] This was in the context of Singapore's post-war years. It was meant to protect tenants from unscrupulous landlords during the post-war housing shortage. In 1953, the Control of Rent Act was enacted. And to cut a long story short, the then-Minister for National Development Mah Bow Tan introduced the Control of Rent (Abolition) Act in 2001.)

Joseph Tan, who shared his memories with me earlier, was born on 22 November 1951. He reflected on his life journey, and his experiences of his childhood home in Aukang, on the occasion of Singapore's 54th National Day—the Singapore Bicentennial year:

> I grew up in my maternal grandfather's land of more than three acres in a part of Lorong Low Koon off Upper Serangoon Road in the 50s and 60s. My childhood years were fun-filled with fond memories of activities in the fold of Mother Nature.
>
> My home then was a two room attap house with a well, without tap water and electricity. The sparse living conditions did not bother me at all as I took them to be the natural order of things then. However, I revelled in the big garden of my house, the lush greeneries amidst coconut, rambutan, durian and other tropical fruit trees on my maternal grandfather's land. These tropical fruit trees provided me and my family with tropical fruits the whole year round![4]

Nature provided a lot of free food! And rambutans were popular in those days. As Robert Yeo remarked to me over lunch, sometimes neighbours would come over and "steal" fruits from his rambutan trees as well. This practice of growing fruits in your own compound was a common one throughout Aukang and in many kampungs around Singapore in the early days.

Those truly were days when people were in close touch with nature.

Utilities: Water, "Bath and Toilet" Facilities, Public Standpipes

Utilities such as tap or piped water were a luxury often not available to many people living in the rural area or provided at great cost. Imagine laying water pipes over long distances to an isolated house. So, the main source of water in the rural area was from wells. Many houses had wells, with some (especially those who were farmers) having more than one. You could also draw water from your neighbours' well with their permission.

A water well. Picture taken in the 1980s. Courtesy of S. Lim.

My father said, "We had to get well water from our neighbours if our well didn't have clear water. My father constructed a cart to carry the tins of water. My brother and I were on water duty. If we were lucky, there would be a pulley and it would be easy to draw water from the well. If not, you had to lower a rope with a pail attached to it first, and then pull the rope up, and that was not be easy."

Wells with pulleys and those without pulleys made a difference in the ease in which water was extracted from the well, especially for children barely ten years old! This could be quite physically challenging and there was always a real risk of falling into the well.

Once the water was extracted, it was still no mean task transporting it from your neighbours' well to your house. My father said that sometimes, when he was pushing the cart with the kerosene tins full of water, heading home, the wheels would get stuck in the sand. To continue moving, he would have to push harder, and some water would splash out of the tins.

Robert Yeo recalled the well at his home at 5 Valley Road:

> **The well, in diameter the equal of my arm spread, was deep, 20 feet down, and water was drawn by a pulley and strong hemp string suspended from a wooden pole. On top of the well was a little hole in the zinc opening to the sky.**
>
> **Before tapped water became available, the well was our only source of water. The well was used for a variety of purposes—washing, cooking, bathing—and it cushioned the impact of droughts. Often we would be told or read about water-rationing in the newspaper and reminded to conserve water because a water-rationing exercise was in place, but with the well, we were protected.**
>
> **What is water rationing to people without modern sanitation?[5]**

There were public standpipes located at strategic locations along major roads—according to my father, there was one at the seventh milestone Upper Serangoon Road. People could go there with pails or empty kerosene tins to collect water and bring it home. Some inconsiderate people "hogged" the standpipe by using it to wash their clothes. Occasionally (if you were lucky) you might even view gratis a guy having a public bath if you happened to walk by or passed by in a bus.

Robert Yeo also described the bath and toilet facilities:

> **The bath area was simply a rectangular area next to the well; in the corner was a base and a tub which was filled with well water when needed. A couple of large nails protruded from the wall space to hold up towels and other clothing while bathing; water was scooped from**

the tub. Females squatted and males pissed and the liquids flowed out into open drains which led to uncemented drains running down beside the bakery to the big canal that was parallel to Tampines Road. The canal must have emptied into the mangrove swamps which began about a kilometer from the intersection where Upper Serangoon meets the Tampines and Punggol Roads. The toilet was a detached, covered small hut at the back of the house; it consisted of a concrete base three feet high with a hole and beneath it was an oval shaped tub which carried the night soil.[6]

An artist's impression of a toilet facility in the 1950s.

My father told me that urine was often passed into a pot and used as fertiliser for plants, and human droppings were often either dropped unceremoniously into a pond if the toilet was built over a pond, or into a bucket or pit for collection, if the toilet was built elsewhere.

Writing about her home at 50A Holy Innocents' Lane, Juliana Teo also shared about the sanitation system of the 1970s:

> At that time, there was no such thing as an ensuite toilet or bathroom. All such amenities were situated outside the house. To bathe, we had to physically pull water with a pail out of the well to fill another pail inside the bathroom. That helped us develop good arm strength. The water was cool and clean. We had to do the same when we wanted to wash our clothes, clean food or even to brush our teeth. The toilets were situated further away to keep the house smelling clean. Can you imagine what it was like at night if you had to do your business? My siblings and I used to look out for each other while one was in the toilet. There was no light leading to the toilet too. Our imagination was activated. Think about doing your business and listening intently to sounds outside the toilet which could signal danger! The person waiting outside was surrounded too by darkness. That used to be our adventure. The older folks were luckier. They had a spittoon in their bedrooms for their relief. This would be emptied the next morning by the night soil carrier. A night soil carrier was a job that those without much choice took on.[7]

A shower facility. Picture taken in the 1980s. Courtesy of S. Lim.

The night soil carrier was also described by Robert Yeo:

> The contents of the tub were cleared every morning, except Sundays, by a night soil person who carried a pole with a tub at each end, both empty. He would pick up the full tub, replace it with an empty one, and when he had two full ones, he sent them to a collection area and went on to the next house. He came early in the morning before I left for school at 7:15am and sometimes later. He was invariably Chinese, wore soiled, grey coolie dress and never looked up.[8]

My father also shared his thoughts on the night soil carrier with me. I found it edifying, but also at the same time quite humorous.

"I honestly do not know how this euphemistic term came about. It has no bearing on reality. The guy worked in the day, not night; and he carried shit, not soil. So, by no stretch of the imagination was he a night soil carrier. I prefer the Teochew term, *tar sai nang*, or the 'person who carries human waste'.

"My mum told me more than once, 'If you don't study hard and fail your exams, you will have to *tar sai*.' I didn't feel offended because during those days, this was what most parents told their sons if they slackened in their studies. Daughters, on the other hand, were threatened differently: 'You had better learn how to cook; if you can't cook, who's going to marry you? Who is going to support you in your old age?'"

Turning his attention back to the topic on the night soil carrier, my father said, "As we didn't have proper sanitation, we emptied our waste into a bucket which was cleaned by the *tar sai nang* twice a week. Once he came when I was squatting over the bucket."

"Oh no," I said.

"For one whole week, I could not eat my meals."

As you can imagine, at the time, the disposal of human waste was genuinely challenging. The flush system, which is taken for granted today, was available only to a lucky—and probably very wealthy—few.

Electricity, Pressure Lamps, and Private Generators

My father shared about his early days without electricity—which was not uncommon in those days.

"Most people in the more remote rural areas didn't have electricity. We could not cook using electricity—in those days we did not have microwave ovens—and so cooking was tough because we had to look for wood, to use as fuel. Charcoal would be better than wood, but unfortunately it was expensive. That is why we needed to use wood and chop it into smaller pieces. To help my family, I would go around the neighbourhood and collect bits and pieces of wood. My friend Boon Kee used to collect wood bark for his family.

"We also did not have a fridge, because we did not have electricity. Instead, we had a larder… with cooked food."

He also told me about pressure lamps and private generators.

"So light was usually powered by a 'pressure lamp'. It needed as fuel a bottle of kerosene costing 20 cents. It was my dad's routine to operate it in the evening. When it was late at night or when he was sleepy he would ask those still awake, 'Do you need the light?' The answer was not given lightly because once total darkness descended on the house it was irreversible as none of us could operate the pressure lamp.

"Some people operated private generators and supplied electricity to households on monthly charges of a flat amount. We made use of such a service when we were living in Jalan Lye Kwee; our immediate neighbours the Chan family did the same. The generator was in the next road, Lorong Batawi."

Transport

"How did you guys get about in those days?" I asked.

"Oh," my father said, "This is an interesting question."

"One mode of transport was the bicycle. For example, my teacher cycled to school; as a student, I often cycled to my grandmother's house, while my friends cycled to school. It was also common for people to use the bicycle to visit their friends and relatives. It was used for practical reasons, rather than recreational reasons like today. It was a necessity."

I thought about my own youth. For me, I only ever cycled for recreational purposes, like going to Telok Kurau Park to play football or cycling along the seaside and reflecting upon life.

My father said, "In those days, there were non-airconditioned taxis. You could bargain or go by metre. What is different today compared to the past is that, back then, we didn't take the taxi from our house, but would walk to the main road to hail one.

"There was also a scheduled taxi service from Upper Serangoon Road sixth milestone to Bras Basah Road. For a group of four people, the fare would be about 30 cents per passenger, making a total of $1.20. Sometimes, when the driver was desperate, he would still drive off with three people.

"We also had the equivalent of Grab and Gojek in those days already! They were called 'pirate taxis'."

"What the heck are pirate taxis?"

"They were literally private cars fetching folks about, just like regular taxis! These were enterprising people who used their own cars to do so, and were unlicensed." exclaimed my father.

My father then shared a random but memorable anecdote with me, which took place in what must have been the early 1970s.

"I was once seated in a pirate taxi, wedged between two fellow passengers, heading back to Aukang.

"One was a vegetable farmer and the other a pig farmer. And they were having a conversation in Teochew, laced with vulgarities, about who made more money. I can still remember part of it. It went something like this."

Vegetable farmer: 'You #$%! pig farmers are so lucky! A #$%! pig can fetch more than $100!'

Pig farmer: 'Lucky? Lucky my #$%!! Do you know how much a #$%! pig eats? It eats non-stop! It's enough to make you bankrupt!'

"And all through the ride, I sat in the middle—amused but silent—as two Teochews argued about whether it was better to be a vegetable or pig farmer."

Well, those were really interesting days with odd taxi conversations.

The government and the unions may have taken a more serious view of pirate taxis. An observation reported in November 1955 was that when there were bus or taxi strikes, it increased the business of the pirate taxi operators.[9]

At the time, competition among pirate taxi operators had become so keen that fares had dropped 10 cents a mile to 5 cents.[10]

In December 1955, the newspaper reported that the Vehicles and Traffic Committee proposed that the City Council pay a reward of 25 percent of the fine imposed upon conviction to those who tipped off Singapore pirate taxi operators.[11] They wanted this move approved as it was difficult to get witnesses prepared to give evidence that would help convict pirate taxi drivers, and an incentive would help the authorities step up enforcement efforts against illegal taxi drivers who were plying openly during the bus strikes and lockout periods. The pirates were cutting into the business of legitimate taxi drivers. As they paid no taxi licence, they charged fares which were competitive with bus rates.

There were some who were sympathetic to the pirate taxi drivers. A writer, going by the pseudonym Sympathy, said that most of these drivers were formerly unemployed and were just trying to make ends meet.[12] He remarked, "The pirate taximen are rather to be pitied than condemned."

All these facts were corroborated by my father. He even said, "They were so important that they could even call strikes."

I looked it up. And it was true!

In March 1966, there was a two-day strike by pirate taxis to protest against impending legislation against them.[13]

Luckily, there were buses and trams in those days. During the 1950s and 60s, there were many bus services in Singapore. The biggest was the Singapore Traction Company, and the rest were 10 local Chinese bus companies.

My father said, "At the time, there was only one bus service, the Punggol Bus Service, plying along Upper Serangoon Road to Kangkar but terminating at Braddell Road and Punggol Point.

Artist's impression of the Punggol Bus Service in the 1950s.

"The bus company was losing money, so the bus drivers were afraid of losing their job. They picked up passengers wherever they were flagged so I could flag them up wherever I wanted.

"At the same time, there was another long-haul bus service, the Singapore Traction Company, which also served Aukang but started from the sixth milestone."

According to Mr Ng Yew Kang, "There used to be a Singapore Traction Company tram service Number 4, that terminated opposite the temple. It went all the way to the General Post Office (GPO) at Fullerton Building (today's Fullerton Hotel) for 25 cents. The markings of the various milestones, such as the fifth or sixth or seventh milestone, are in relation to the GPO."

When it came to roads at the time, many smaller roads were mud tracks, with puddles of water when it rained. This meant that drivers had to drive in a zigzag manner to avoid pockets of uneven ground. In contrast, major public roads were "proper" bitumen roads.

My father said, "In those days, many families didn't have cars, but farmers often did. Cars were used for business rather than for personal use. Sometimes these farmers had motorbikes with a side carriage."

Sometimes, cars could get stuck in the mud.

"Most of the mud roads or lanes had potholes and cars could get stuck in them when their tyres went into them. Drivers who were stuck needed to depend on others to help them push their cars out. Sometimes we felt sorry for them and helped out.

"If your car were stuck, the worst thing to do was to ram the accelerator. However, that is precisely what they often did. The problem is that when you rammed the accelerator, the tyres would spin without the car moving forward. Instead, mud would fly and splatter all over the folks who were trying to help.

"I remember once this happened, during the Christmas season when we were at Jalan Payoh Lai. There was a kind gentleman who drove into the side lane, and presented my father with a lot of goodies. However, when he was driving out of Jalan Payoh Lai, his car got stuck in a muddy pothole. We were grateful to him for the gifts and wanted to help him, so we ran over to assist. And we ended up getting muddy when he rammed his accelerator!"

My father continued, "Eventually, private roads were turned into public roads. For example, when I was young, Jalan Lye Kwee was originally a private mud track in the late 50s. Eventually, it was turned into a public tar road. The government upgraded the private roads in stages and made all the residents pay for them. How

My Father's Kampung

much you paid was determined by the length of your frontage.

"However, the moment the mud tracks were turned into bitumen roads, they were gazetted by the government as public roads. If they were left as private roads, the people who lived there could stop other citizens from using the road, deny them access. And the state could not allow that."

Clearly, today's transport network is a lot more modern, coordinated, and better connected.

Entertainment

My father also told me of all the fun he had when he was a youth.

"In the 1950s, I had a catapult to shoot birds on trees. Basically, we were too young to qualify for an air rifle then, so we used the next best thing. We made it ourselves. All my friends and neighbours also did the same thing. We used it mainly to shoot birds, mudskippers, sea snakes, and miniature crabs called *bua kee*. Sometimes, when I shot a bird, it would land on the roof of a person's house, pong! The neighbours would hear the loud noise, and come out, and we would run away."

I laughed. This was comedy gold.

"However, shooting birds was often for food. Whenever I shot a bird, I would bring it home for Mum to cook. And whenever my friend John shot a bird, he would bring it home for his servant to cook.

"But shooting birds was not without its costs.

"If the bird was in the tree and we missed it and hit the branch instead, the stone would ricochet and might hit us. If the birds were in flight and we shot at them, the stone might land anywhere.

"Once, two stones landed with a loud bang almost simultaneously on the zinc roof

Kampung children playing with marbles in the 1950s. Photo by the late Harold Arozoo; courtesy of Edmund M Arozoo.

of a house. There was an outraged shout of 'Hey' and a furious man came charging out. Both John and I ran for dear life!"

Crocodiles, a Bear, and a Python

My father said, "In the late 1960s, I gave tuition to a boy, whose father ran a crocodile farm at Aukang. I taught him English in his kitchen, for $30 a month."

"What? I mean, I can believe you gave tuition, but what crocodile farm are you talking about?" I asked.

He told me the true story of a crocodile farm at Upper Serangoon Road.

Tan Moh Hong Reptile Skin and Crocodile Farm (Singapore Crocodile Farm) was located along Upper Serangoon Road.

Tan Moh Hong Reptile Skin and Crocodile Farm. Courtesy of S. Lim.

The crocodile farm at Upper Serangoon Road was the only one of its kind in Singapore when it was established after the end of World War II by Tan Gua Chua to share his fascination with crocodiles with the public.[14] Located on a 90,000 square feet site on the outskirts of the Serangoon Garden Estate, the farm produced crocodile skins for Tan's tannery firm to make shoes, wallets, belts, and handbags. In the 1960s, the farm was managed by Tay Ghee Pang, whose job was to feed the crocodiles at the farm daily and to capture at least 100 of the reptiles every month for skinning. By the 1970s, the farm had developed into a popular tourist attraction where tourists could view live crocodiles, most of which were imported from Indonesia and Cambodia. Next to the farm was a factory where visitors could view tanning and processing and a shop where they could purchase finished crocodile skin products. Its popularity inspired a crocodilarium at East Coast Parkway and a crocodile park at Jurong Hill in the 1980s.

In 1972, the crocodile farm received much media publicity when Lord Louis Mountbatten (1900–1979) paid a private visit to the farm with his family.

Tan Gna Chua passed away in 2000 at an age of 85, leaving behind an estimated $30 million worth of assets.[15]

My father said, "It has to be said that, in Aukang, beyond the historical Punggol Zoo and the crocodile farm, people often kept whatever pets they wanted as their neighbours never complained. In the 1960s, it was already illegal to keep dangerous and wild animals as pets, but people were more easy-going then.

"Once Ku Luk, an uncle, kept a bear. Nobody knew where he got it from, but most probably he bought it from a friend. He built a big and strong cage to keep it. But the bear escaped and when he tried to capture it, he was mauled. He only decided to get rid of the beast one day when the bear bit his wife, Ah Kheng.

"Another family reared a giant python in a big cage; it was like a one-animal zoo with visitors dropping over uninvited to admire it. Sometimes, on my way home from school, I would do just that."

Well, it looks like people in Singapore's early days were a lot more in tune with nature and animals than they are today.

Badminton Parties

My father is crazy about badminton.

Once, he challenged me to a badminton match at Kembangan Community Centre.

Thinking that I could not lose to a much older gentleman, I foolishly accepted this challenge.

He duly beat me and I never played badminton with him ever again. But one question intrigued me: why was my father so crazy about badminton?

My father replied, "Well, I started playing 'badminton' using an exercise book as a racquet and a match box as a shuttlecock. Then I graduated to the real thing using borrowed racquets and shuttlecocks discarded by the adult players, which were often so badly damaged that they were unreliable in their flight paths, spinning like a propeller when hit. And at first, I would only play when the adults had their break.

"Open-air badminton courts were found all over the country. The humble unsurfaced sand and clay court in front of Ah Ma's house was the scene of many a great badminton battle. In Jalan Lye Kwee, where we lived many years later, Peng Kiang had the best badminton court; it was professionally constructed with a cement floor and proper lighting. Unfortunately, it was exclusively for his family's use.

"The court in the backyard of Enche Abdullah's house with a sand and clay surface, but with proper lighting, was available to the neighbours. The court in Ah Kim's house 'constructed' by us and Liam's communist friend, Hiok Ngee, was the worst. It was used by our family and friends."

I said, "Robert Yeo also shared with me that there was also a junior badminton club in 7 Valley Road, next to his house in 5 Valley Road at Lak Kor. Badminton was very popular. Did you have any favourite sports stars then?"

My father said, "Oh, we had our local favourite badminton 'stars', calling them Tan Joe Hock, Ferry Sonneville, and Charoen Wattanasin, the badminton heroes of the 1960s. The first two were top Indonesian players while the third was Thailand's best singles player. And of course, if you were older, you would hero-worship Wong Peng Soon. But in the 1960s, I thought that he was already a has-been."

Speaking with me over coffee at Keppel Club, Lee Tong Juan also shared stories about the 'badminton parties' held not just in Aukang, but all over Singapore, in bygone days in the 1950s to 1980s. He said animatedly, recalling fond days:

> Badminton was a popular sport back then. It was the craze for the boys in my neighbourhood. The radio was the only source of news for the much-publicised Thomas Cup tournaments where the Singapore/Malaya team clinched the inaugural Thomas Cup in 1949 and retained it in 1952 and 1955. We enjoyed listening to the Caucasian commentator providing a running commentary on every match.
>
> My neighbour Edwin Choo, an Anglo-Chinese School (ACS) boy, played badminton with me. Later on, I played with the Kang brothers who were my Teochew neighbours at Florence Road. The

Kang family was well-to-do, and had one acre of land, and even allowed us to build a house. I had no formal training in badminton, but learnt from my Teochew neighbours. One example of an interesting badminton technique was the "crocodile service", pioneered by Ong Poh Lim, and which we tried to master.

Local badminton enthusiasts often got together to form parties to play the game and I was no exception. In Aukang alone, there were many badminton parties. I was in many of them, namely the Rainbow badminton party (in Upper Serangoon Road), Crescent badminton party (in Paya Lebar Crescent), Flower badminton party (in Flower Road), and Maybud badminton party. In those days, we could join multiple badminton parties. One of the most popular badminton parties was the Mayflower badminton party. Also, I had the privilege of being nominated by my school to be coached by the famous badminton player, Wong Peng Soon, at Victoria School.

Wealthy businessmen and prominent personalities were usually made presidents of the badminton parties. And an interesting fact might be that, before he became the President of Singapore, Wee Kim Wee was already a president … of the Crescent Badminton party!

I used to play badminton four or five times a week, normally after dinner, around 7pm. Using kerosene pressure lamps to light up the court, we would play the game into the night.

In those days, with no indoor courts, we were at the mercy of the elements. There were days we had to sit out strong winds and get really busy after a downpour. With gunny sacks, we would mop up the rainwater on sandy courts or concrete cement ones in big compound houses of wealthy businessmen.

Inter-party friendly games on Saturdays drew many spectators; some with genuine interest in the game, others for quiet betting purposes.

By the 1980s, interest in badminton dissipated when the sports scene became more dynamic, and there were many alternatives to badminton. The game declined and standards fell.

That was a pity. But this also explained why my father was amazing at badminton—the whole community was crazy about it, and they played a lot. And the kampung spirit meant that you could just walk into anyone's compound and watch a match going on.

Movies in the 1950s and 60s

But badminton was not the only interesting pastime. Movies were already a big thing too. One day, my father told me about how they watched movies in the past.

"We used to watch free movies when we were living in Jalan Payoh Lai. One of the matriarchs in the neighbourhood was called Tua Cher Neo (big lady Cher). She and her family lived in a large house and would screen movies in the half-walled porch of their house. If she knew you, she might invite you in to watch the movie with her and her family."

"And what if she didn't know you personally?" I asked.

"Well, in that case, you would have to watch from outside the compound of the house and you might have to look at the screen at an awkward angle. I was one of the uninvited guests watching from outside the house. And I had to stand all the time, so honestly it was not a very satisfactory way of watching a movie.

"Later, we found a much better and more comfortable way to watch movies. But it cost 10 cents and we had to walk a few kilometres from Jalan Payoh Lai to Punggol Road. The screen was much bigger and tied between two coconut trees. Since there were no chairs, we sat on the grass using our slippers to protect our shorts from being soiled. We would pray for good weather. If it rained, the screening would be cancelled without any refund.

"When Montfort School screened third-run movies to raise funds, we received a boost in our standard of living. We were happy! We could now watch movies in a proper seat with a fan twirling overhead. But it cost 20 cents for normal seats and 30 cents for gallery seats.

"And there was an additional irritant. Since only one projector was used, this meant that if the movie had three reels of film there would be two 'intermissions'. On top of that, when the screen came on again the image might sometimes appear upside down because the reel was fixed the wrong way. The missionary brothers certainly had piety, but they did not necessarily have the technical skills in screening a movie!"

"Bless their souls," we said in unison.

"Having said that," my father said, "there were also other ways of enjoying movies at Aukang. There was the Empire Theatre at the junction of Lowland Road and Upper Serangoon Road at the sixth milestone, and Mercury Theatre at Sirat Road at the fifth milestone. For Teochew and Chinese movies, there was also Kok Wah Theatre.

"These were 'kampung cinemas' and showed only second or even third-run movies, after they had been screened elsewhere in Singapore. But well, the cinema tickets were cheaper. That was the order of things at the time. We didn't feel deprived; we didn't feel sorry for ourselves."

I said, "Interestingly, Robert Yeo mentioned to me that the seats at the cinemas were sometimes infested with bugs, but they still went there anyways. There were also enormous queues for popular movies, and one memory which stood out for him was his cousin putting his arm into the box office waving his money, and shouting at the teller, 'Take my money!'[16]

"Robert also told me about the monthly *Movie News*, and said that he would eagerly wait for each edition to come out."

As Robert Yeo wrote in *Routes*:

> *Movie News* was a glossy monthly which carried news and what's more, black-and-white and colour pictures of movie stars in innocent romantic proximity or in action. In addition, there were full one-page portraits of the famous, the glamorous and the handsome. Nothing, in those days, gave me more pleasure than anticipating and then buying a new monthly copy of *Movie News* and [sic] from the Chinese man dressed in a white, sleeveless singlet who set up a simple square table in the parking lot of the Empire Theatre.[17]

My father said, "Yes, I remember reading *Movie News* too. It carried articles not only of Westerns and American movies, but also of Chinese and Malay movies from the Shaw Brothers. And I remember that the Catholic Church would publish ratings on the movies—this movie had no objectionable content, while that one had objectionable content. Devout Catholics in Aukang would have taken those ratings seriously.

"However, one day, your Kong Kong (grandfather) set out to defeat the Empire. Not the British Empire, but Empire Theatre, the cinema.[18]

"Ah Pa and his drinking buddy, a Chinaman contractor by the puzzling name of Amat, and a number of joint venture partners decided to bring the Empire down to its knees by capturing the cinema market and undercutting the Empire's pricing. They actually managed to build a rudimentary cinema on a plot of vacant land near Banana Grove. Their cineplex consisted of an open-air enclosure surrounded by corrugated zinc sheets. Their pricing was half the price of the Empire's, at 15 cents versus the princely sum of 30 cents.

"I remember Ah Pa was so elated, predicting the downfall of the Empire, after which he would take on Mercury down the road.

"Ah Ma and Liam (my father's nickname for my uncle, William) attended the premier, which featured a cowboy film. Ah Pa was the projector operator. It was a fiasco right from the start because the projector kept on breaking down. Ah Pa kept on swearing and cursing, and calling for his partner: Amat! Amat! The crowd hissed and booed. Finally, the cineplex had no choice but to refund the audience.

"Unsurprisingly and rather unfortunately, the whole operation closed shop subsequently, after being besieged by numerous problems."

Gambling

"Gambling was also a common pastime in those days," my father said. "For example, my grandmother, mother, and uncles and aunties gambled almost every Saturday and Sunday, as well as on festive occasions like Christmas and Chinese New Year.

"Shorter sessions would usually start after lunch and end before dinner. The longer sessions would last the whole day with a break for meals, and some marathon sessions would extend until the next day. Sometimes there were two or three concurrent sessions, confined to the family members and the occasional close friends. The games played were usually mahjong, *see sake* (four colours card game) and occasionally *cher kee* (also spelt cherki, a more complicated version of *see sake*). When it came to mahjong, most of my cousins picked up the intricacies of the game, but surprisingly my brothers and I never learned how to play it."

I simply had to find out more about what these gambling games.

My father explained, "Popular worldwide, mahjong is a tile-based game developed in China during the Qing. Commonly played by four players, sometimes three, it has regional variants. Mahjong is essentially a game of skill, strategy, and calculation, but involves a degree of chance. Singapore mahjong is unique, with its set of rules and regulations (for example, animals are involved as tai; the game ends at the last 15 tiles; and stakes are increased geometrically)."[19]

"What about *see sake*?" I asked.

My father explained, "*See sake pai*, literally 'four colour cards', more commonly known simply as *see sake*, was a favourite Teochew card game popular among housewives. In this game, 112 cards are divided into four colours (yellow, red, white, and green), 28 cards each. In each colour, the cards are listed as General, Guard, Advisor, Chariot, Horse, Cannon, and Pawn, much like Chinese chess."[20]

"But these weren't the only games, correct?" I asked.

"Much later when my Ah Ma had passed on, Mum found her real love: playing *See Gee* (four numbers), which were illegal four-digit lucky draws organised by syndicates. You could buy *Tua Gee* (big numbers) which entitled you to only the top prizes; or the 'normal numbers' which also offered consolation prizes (*bear sai* or horse shit) as well. And there were *Ang Gee* (red numbers), where only limited bets were allowed. These were popular numbers that many people might place a bet on and had to be limited to prevent the syndicates from being wiped out if the numbers turned out to be winners!"

"The diversity of gambling pastimes was incredible!" I said.

My father continued, "But that's not all. There was also an enterprising hawker who sold *lo ark* (braised duck) in Lorong Low Koon. The deal was a whole duck for $2, half for $1, and a quarter for 50 cents.

"But he would give you the option of getting free food. You could stake your money against his duck at the same rate. If you bet $1 and won, you would get half a duck; if you bet $1 and lost, he would keep his duck. It was decided by tossing two dices in a best of three game."

My father laughed.

"I loved to watch this. From my keen sense of observation, in this 'game of chance', the loser was usually the customer."

"Oh, how was Ah Ma's and Kong Kong's luck when it came to gambling, by the way?" I asked, curious.

My father chuckled, "Mum's luck wasn't too good, but Pa's luck was better. Most of the time he won although occasionally he had a spell of what he termed as 'arse luck'!

"We would know that he had won when we saw him returning home with one or two packets of *mee* or *kway teow*."

Suddenly, his tone changed. "Gambling was everywhere. But I also witnessed an act of intimidation and violence in public. Once, I was walking home from school when I came across a number of people squatting under a tree, gambling. At the time, gambling often took place under trees because people sat on the roots and took shelter from the sun by sitting in the shade. So, I went nearer to watch.

"Suddenly, there was a frightful commotion and someone was punched repeatedly by an assailant screaming loudly in Hokkien, 'You cannot stop just like that! You must give *lim pei* (your father) a chance to win my money back!'

"I did not stay to find out what happened next!"

Fighting Fish and Other Animals

"If I remember correctly, you were also interested in fighting fish," I said. "Remember how you used to keep them at home when we were living in Joo Chiat?"

My father replied, "Yes, in those days we also kept fighting fish as a hobby.

"After my fourth uncle picked up keeping fighting fish as a hobby, I would walk all the way from Jalan Lye Kwee to Lorong Low Koon with my 'first king' to challenge his 'first king'. Invariably, however, my fish lost. Later, I realised why—it was traumatised and exhausted by the long journey and was incapable of putting up a good fight!

"Actually, anyone could just set up his own aquarium and fish farm in those days. In fact, that is what they did.

"For those who were so inclined, they could set up a dog centre—what we would call a canine centre these days—and breed pedigree dogs for sale. If you wanted a dog, you'd go over to your neighbour's house and ask for one. Sometimes, he'd give one to you, if you were a good friend.

"Living near dog breeders required a lot of patience and tolerance as the dogs would be barking all the time. This required a true kampung spirit—you tolerated the noise and other irritants because you knew that your neighbour was just trying to earn a living. It was about being neighbourly."

Banning Firecrackers Long Before the Government Did

"We had the Bee Tee family as our neighbours. They had a house flanked by two other houses on either side, all fenced up with the front gate facing one road, Jalan Lye Kwee, and the back gate facing another, Lorong Batawi. That was how Bee Tee and his multi-generational families lived.

"One of Bee Tee's greatest fears was that his house would be burnt down during the Chinese New Year period. His next greatest fear was that one of his neighbours' houses would also be burnt down. But his second fear was not due to concern for their welfare. Rather, it was due to his first fear.

"Yes, the firecrackers might land on his house and start a large fire. But even if the firecrackers landed on his neighbours' houses instead, the wind might still blow the fire to his house. So it was all the same whether the firecrackers had hit his house or his neighbours' houses!

"As most of the houses were made of wood and some had attap roofs, this fear was reasonable. In fact, in those days, every Chinese New Year brought the same calamities: houses being burnt down and people being made homeless or hurt by exploding firecrackers. So Bee Tee banned firecrackers long before the government did.

"But Pa was defiant and regarded him as crazy, and told us to ignore him (*mai chap siow yee*). So we joined in the festivities each Chinese New Year and I had a nice time defying Bee Tee. He would glare at me, but didn't dare to stop me."

Teochew Opera

There was an array of exciting Teochew opera street performances. As my father did not watch much Teochew opera when he was young, I went to look for someone who did. I had the good fortune of talking to Ng Yew Kang, who—while not being much of a fan—watched enough Teochew opera to tell me about how it was like at Aukang.

Sitting in his beautiful home, I asked, "Did you watch Teochew opera?"

Mr Ng said, "I watched Teochew opera at temples near my house when there were celebrations. A temporary stage would be set up, probably around once a year. The opera would last for three to four days and was quite popular. People would bring their own wooden benches which could seat two or three, or chairs. They would go early to ensure getting a vantage point immediately in front of the stage. You had to stand if you didn't bring a chair or bench. I wasn't a fan, but I did watch the opera for some time and then went to eat the titbits sold by the hawkers.

"Around the site of the opera, there were hawkers selling drinks; dried cuttlefish (*jiu her*) grilled over charcoal fire, with hammers used to beat it to make it less tough, and people ate the *jiu her* with prawn paste and chili sauce; *rojak*; *tau kwa pao* stuffed with *tao gey* and cucumber, grilled over small stoves filled with charcoal, and eaten with prawn paste and chili; cockles (*hum*) in a small bowl, which were boiled and eaten on the spot.

"The standard of the local Chinese Opera troupes was not very high. By comparison, the troupe from Hongkong with Ms Tan Chor Hwee as the main actress attracted a much more enthusiastic crowd. I came to really appreciate Teochew Opera when the Shantou First Teochew Opera Troupe came to perform at the then-National Theatre for the first time in the early 1970s. They were so good that the

3,470-seat National Theatre was fully packed for up to 15 performances. People queued up to buy tickets from the National Theatre to part of River Valley Road."

"Wow," I said. Suddenly, Mr Ng brought up the Tou Mu Kung Temple, referring to its more common name in Teochew.

"The fifth milestone Kow Ong Yah Temple used to hold nine days of celebrations with Teochew opera. It was held on the first day to the ninth day, of the ninth moon in the Lunar calendar.

"The Teochew wayang was held at the permanent stage in front of the temple for nine days. People would pray at the temple—parents would bring their children. They would have to cross a bridge, after which, the folks at the temple would chop a red seal on the back of your shirt and tie a yellow cloth band around the right wrist, to indicate that you had come to the temple and were blessed by the deity. It was very crowded during the nine days."

I nodded excitedly. My father had told me this story earlier.

Corroborating what my father said on a different occasion, Mr Ng said, "There was a massive procession all the way to and from Punggol Point. The devotees would receive the deity from the sea on the first day of the ninth moon from Punggol Point, then go back all the way to the temple. On the ninth day, there would be another procession to send the deity back to the sea. It was another big procession, with gongs, a sedan chair, and lorries. It was the most popular event in this area and the crowd was huge. While the festival is still celebrated today, it is not as big as it was in the past."

This was an incredible and personal sharing. It suggested to me that Teochew opera was not just cultural, but also tied closely to religion, through the temple activities. But this also implied that as times changed and the modern generation associated less and less with the culture and temple activities in general, then there would be correspondingly less interest. This further suggested that there had to be a change in the way these arts and cultural forms were performed, so that they could be more relevant to people today.

As Paul Tan, then-Deputy Chief Executive Officer of the National Arts Council (NAC) rightly said in 2015 of traditional arts and Teochew opera:

> **How are such traditions relevant to Singaporean youth today? Contemporising the art form, while respecting its heritage, isn't easy—but surely this could also be an opportunity, challenging the**

> more ready groups to innovate? It could even build new bridges to other ethnic and language groups, and expand audiences.
>
> The truth is that, without a community to draw energy from, productions—no matter how professionally staged—will play to empty houses.[21]

Artist's impression of Teochew opera in the 1950s, depicting "One Household, Three Scholars", a Teochew play where a father and his two sons passed the imperial examinations and became scholars.

Eking Out a Living

My father told me that life was tough in the old days, so people did whatever they could to survive. Basically, many people living in the kampungs were farmers, often making their living from pig or poultry farming.

My father said, "In Lorong Low Koon and later in Jalan Payoh Lai, we were surrounded by farmers. Ah Buck Chek, a pig farmer, was a kind man who allowed us to draw water from his well. However, I sometimes shudder to think of the 'clear water' we drew from Ah Buck Chek's well which we used for drinking. The pigsty was next to the well. Living among farmers brought us little benefit but inflicted on us a huge cost. We got the stench but never a free chicken; all farm produce was for sale."

This was a clear example of the economics concept of negative externalities, spillover effects on third parties not involved in the production or consumption of a good.

"In Lorong Low Koon the farmers were Ah Ee-ah, who reared mainly ducks and chickens, and Poh Kim, who reared pigs. Ah Ee-ah worked very hard, but died before he could enjoy the fruits of his labour, something his wife lamented on at his funeral. My mother found the widow's remark poignant and repeated it to me many times, so much so that I can remember it more than 50 years on: *boh chiat ko hor, du see ker* (meaning that the unfortunate gentleman died before he could eat something good)."

Life was not always good in the good old days.

Later when my father moved to Jalan Payoh Lai, he observed pastoral farming at a closer range and at a more mature age. Two farmers stood out in his memory, Ol Ter (Black Pig) and Buck Chek (Uncle Buck).

My father said: "Like most farmers, Ol Ter did not hatch his own chicks. He bought them from a shop specialising in the sale of chicks, ducklings, goslings and other infant animals which in turn bought them from a hatchery. As it would take 15–16 weeks to raise chicks for slaughter, Ol Ter could raise at least three flocks of chickens a year, the biggest coinciding with the Chinese New Year.

"He would convert his master bedroom into a chicken nursery and turn it into a fortress. All the furniture—bed, cupboard, everything—would be shifted out of the room. The cement floor would then be covered with gunny sack. The windows would be securely fastened and the door locked. Every tiny open space where a rat or a cat—the biggest enemies of chicks—could come in would be sealed.

"His wife would sleep elsewhere and he would sleep with the chicks. Imagine him sleeping in a collapsible canvas bed with 1,000 to 1,500 chicks running about below him. He would do this for a month before he felt confident to move the young chickens to an open-air enclosure to forage. In the evening he would move them to the safety of a strongly fortified hen house.

"Even then he could not sleep in peace. If the chickens clucked loudly it would mean that something was disturbing them. It could be a cat; or worse, it could be a thief trying to steal his chickens. You can understand his relief when the chickens were fully grown and the wholesaler came to take the burden off his shoulders.

"With thousands of chickens and ducks living in a confined space, there was bound to be some fighting among them. So how did he deal with conflicts among his poultry? He tolerated no nonsense. Once I was watching an aggressive duck pecking the other ducks that went near it.

"Suddenly, Ol Ter grabbed hold of the aggressor by the neck. With his other hand, he pried open the duck's beak, and using his teeth, bit off two rows of teeth from the duck, and effectively made the duck toothless."

I shuddered, speechless.

My father continued: "Ol Ter also had three ponds on his farms. He would drive his ducks or ducklings to the pond for a daily swim. The pond was a good way to drown a dog that was too old. One would force the unlucky fella into an elongated pig cage made of cane, and then submerge the cage into the water for a few minutes using bamboo poles.

"Ol Ter grew water hyacinth and *kang kong* in the ponds. Water hyacinth provided food for the pigs when cooked with swill that the pigs liked. *Kang kong* would be cooked with home-grown chili padi and served at the dinner table. He also reared fish like tilapia (*jee-pun her*) and the snakehead (tioman or *loi her*) which provided his family with a good source of protein."

"How about Ah Buck Chek?" I asked.

My father replied, "He was a pig farmer. But he did not have his own boar for stud services. One memory that stands out for me was that one day, his stepson Boon Teck, invited me over to his house to 'watch something interesting'.

"His father had arranged for stud services for one of his sows; a man was going to bring a boar to mate with one of the farm's sows.

"When it was show time, I was amazed.

"In the midst of Ah Buck Chek's daughters' giggling, the boar had no shame and did what was expected of him!"

Private School

We might think of private tuition as something that only came about much later in Singapore's history. However, private lessons and tuition go way back in our history, even in the 1950s.

My father said, "Life was tough in the old days, so people did whatever they could to survive. One of our neighbours, a young man called Ah Tuck, set up a 'school' near Ah Ma's house. He didn't even have an O level qualification but that did not prevent him from starting his school. Building an 'open-air' shed beside his parents' house, he equipped it with a blackboard, lots of chalk, a long ruler, a few home-made tables and benches and he was in business.

"The school was at 'primary' level catering to those in regular schools but needing

Kampung Memories (1946–1975)

additional coaching. It was actually the forerunner of our later concept of private tuition centres, except that Ah Tuck ran it like a school. For example, the students had to call him 'Sir' and wish him 'Good morning'.

"Among the students he attracted was a future government scholar who rose to be the PWD's Chief Quantity Surveyor in Singapore!"

Travelling Hawkers or Street Hawkers

One part of the economy was the travelling hawkers of the time. Hawking actually refers to going from place to place to sell; it often meant being at a given place along a street without a licence or not paying rent. So technically the term hawker centre, applied today, is a kind of paradox—it implies stationary itinerant hawkers.

On the supply side, why were there so many hawkers? One possible reason was that unemployment was high in the post-war days. Unemployment was estimated to be 10 percent (or 46,000) of the labour force in 1959, and with the post-war babies coming into the labour market, even greater unemployment was predicted in the 1960s, and an estimated 84,000 jobs were required.[22] People did what they had to survive. Salaries were low so families had to find many ways to feed themselves.

On the demand side, it's quite clear why there was demand for street hawkers. They served an important need and kept people fed and supplied.

An artist's impression of an itinerant street hawker.

Dr John Kwok wrote an interesting piece on "How Singapore's hawker culture started" which came out on 3 April 2019. I enjoyed reading it:

> Street hawkers appeared in Singapore almost immediately when the British established a port on the island in 1819...
>
> The big change came in 1970 when the Singapore government announced that all licensed hawkers would be cleared off the streets over the next five years.
>
> The Housing Development Board (HDB) started building hawker centres across Singapore, and the 24,845 licensed street hawkers would finally have clean and hygienic stalls to work in...
>
> It was the resettlement of street hawkers from the city to the HDB estates that made hawker centres "community dining rooms" in an urban setting, and a key characteristic that make up hawker culture in Singapore.
>
> Hawker centres ended street hawkers in Singapore and what emerged after the 1970s is a hawker culture that is familiar and celebrated in Singapore. As Singapore puts up Hawker Culture as its nomination to UNESCO, it is important to know how it all started.[23]

Singaporeans love food. It is an integral part of our DNA. And before they were resettled into HDB estates, these street hawkers were ready to peddle a whole range of foods literally on the streets—such as ready food like *soon kway, monk kwang kuay, koo chai kway, otah kway*, bread and kaya, bread and butter, ice cream, *kacang putih*, braised duck; and mobile, on-the-spot cooked food like satay, wanton noodles, and *char kway teow*.

Lugging along all the accoutrements, such as a frying pan, pots, firewood, and a pail of water using a pole on the shoulder, the street hawker—and if he was married, his wife would join him too—serve customers by the side of the road. My father shared his memories of the street hawkers at Aukang.

"I will always remember the *kor loh mee* man for three reasons. First, once a dog attacked him, and in order to escape, he ran into our garden and fell down.

"Second, he worked every single day, but once—just once—he didn't turn up. That was the day he got married. The next day, he was back, with his wife as his helper.

"Third, I bargained with him. The *mee* soup was 20 cents but the *tar mee* was 30 cents. Despite having only 20 cents, I asked for *tar mee*. He agreed, but I had to forgo the *wanton* and *char siew*.

"From then onwards, I always ordered *tar mee* for 20 cents, sans *wanton* and *char siew*!

"I remember being scolded by the *soon kueh* seller. Once, I was in St Xavier's Lane when I called out to her to come over to Jalan Lye Kwee, the lane near to it. When she came over and found out that I only wanted to buy two *soon kueh*, of five cents each, she told me off. 'You asked me to come all the way for 10 cents? You think your 10 cents is *gu chia leng* (bullock cart wheel, or something very valuable)?'

"There was a *kacang putih* man, a big Indian man dressed in white, who would always station himself strategically outside my neighbour's house at Jalan Lye Kwee, instead of moving about. He never ever called out: *kacang putih! Kacang putih!* Instead, he would shout: Yip! Yip! That was the signal.

"A paper cone of nuts cost five cents. If I could afford it, which was hardly ever, I would buy 10 cashew nuts for 10 cents.

"I always thought 'Yip Yip' was a nice and kind man until the day I saw him threatening to beat up a hapless competitor who had encroached on his territory. This was his *kacang putih* turf. Well, I suppose he had to defend it out of economic necessity.

"Incidentally, Ah Ma used 'Yip Yip' to teach us a lesson on saving. He only got five cents at a time, and yet he could save enough to go back to India, get married, and buy a house.

"The lesson was lost on me, as I was a young man then. I had no intention of going to India, getting married, or buying a house!"

My father continued, "Hawking is more than just selling cooked food. In those days, people sold everything. I have fond memories of a street hawker, called Ah La, a 'social unifier'. He was a fishmonger, who used to come by on his bicycle with his stock of fish from Kangkar fish market. The neighbours would come out of their houses and congregate, and while they selected fish for lunch and dinner, they would socialise and exchange gossip. Eventually, he became a family friend.

"We had two big guava trees and, in season, there would be hundreds of ripe guava fruits. Once, Ah Ma requested his help to climb our trees and pluck our fruits, to sell them for us. He kindly agreed and climbed up the tree to help collect the fruits. Ah Pa did not know about this arrangement, and so when he came home one day and saw Ah La plucking our fruits, he scolded him! Poor fellow. And the best part was that he was helping us out of friendship! To me, this is the true kampung spirit."

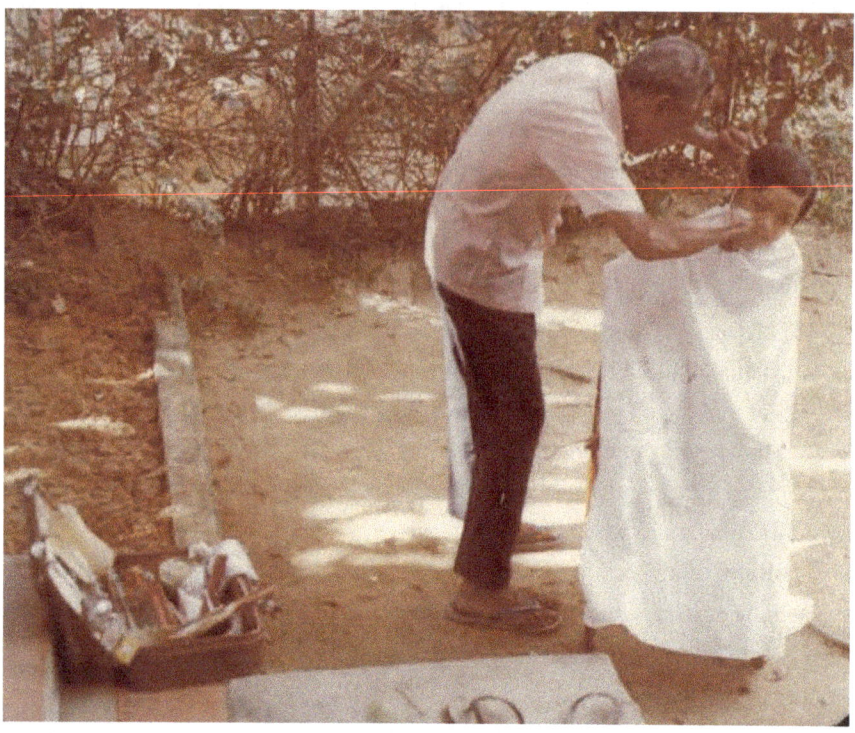

A mobile barber in the 1970s. Courtesy of Encik Salleh Sariman.

Commercial Farming

My father said, "There were certain common practices by non-farmers: rearing poultry, especially chickens and ducks, for one's own consumption especially for festive seasons, growing vegetables (*kang kong*, tapioca), and planting fruit trees (guava, papaya, rambutan). And the biggest festive season would be Chinese New Year. Often, live chickens and ducks were given as presents before Chinese New Year."

But Aukang also had a history of commercial farming, where several neighbours were in fact growing vegetables, rearing livestock, and fishing (mostly at Kangkar and Punggol) for commercial reasons. Before independence, and for a few years after, farmers in Aukang were able to rear both chickens and pigs (and hence, my father could witness interesting chicken versus pig farming conversations while taking a pirate taxi in the early 1970s).

An artist's impression of a Punggol pig farm.

However, Aukang's commercial pig farmers were first relocated to Punggol in the 1970s. This resettlement impacted poultry farmers' economic fortunes as well. Then-Vice-President of the Singapore Livestock Farmers Association Mr Leow Leong Poh once said that, in the past, when the prices of eggs fell below cost, farmers could easily switch to rearing more pigs to offset their losses.[24] However, in the late 1970s, this was not possible because those who reared pigs had been resettled in Punggol and Jalan Kayu, and those who reared poultry in Lim Chu Kang.

Leow Leong Poh was also company chairman of the Singapore Eggs and Poultry Trading Ltd, founded in September 1978, which represented about 60 percent of the about 400 poultry farmers in Singapore.[25] It collected eggs from its about 200 members in Punggol, Chua Chu Kang, Lim Chu Kang, and Jurong and supplied them to retailers regularly at a constant price. It bought eggs from farmers according to weight, at $2.12 per kg, instead of the common 10-piece system. It had a factory in Jurong with eight machines, costing about $4,000 each, to sort the eggs according to size for distribution to retailers.

But despite the pig and poultry farmers' best efforts, in the end, the writing was on the wall. In the 1980s, pig farms were gradually phased out to be replaced with high-tech, non-pollutive farming and aquaculture.[26]

In 1984, then-Chairman of the Singapore Livestock Farmers' Association Leow

Leong Poh, representing 592 members, said in a coordinated response that there was a need to maintain Singapore's pig and poultry farming to ensure Singapore's wellbeing, and that they had a role to play in society.[27] This was in response to then-DPM Goh Keng Swee's policy statements in Parliament on the possible phasing out of pig, poultry, and vegetable farms in Singapore, as there were no plans for Singapore to be self-sufficient in pork, poultry, or eggs, and that Singapore should focus on earning its income producing goods and providing services. The Association countered by arguing that supplementing domestic production with imports was practical, rather than relying entirely upon imports. There was concern about not having stable supply sources. Chicken farmers in 1984 were already supplying about 80 percent of local demand and pig farmers were on track to produce 85 percent of Singapore's pork requirements in 1985. Ancillary services such as feedmillers and transport services would be affected by the plans to phase out farming. And as for pollution from pig farms, Toh Joo Ee, the Vice Chairman of the pig farmers sub-committee argued that there were plans to install expensive waste treatment plants at the farms.

There were 354 pig-rearing members of the Singapore Livestock Farmers' Association in 1984.[28]

The phasing out of pig farming affected many local businesses in Singapore, including one which would later on become quite famous.[29] The beginnings of Qian Hu go back to the 1980s when Kenny Yap's father, Yap Tik Huay, and his brother, Yap Hey Cha, ran a pig farm in Sembawang, rearing pigs as a family business.

During that time, however, the Singapore government was in the midst of making efforts to relocate and eventually wipe out all pig farms in the country not only because of the pollution they were causing, but also to make room for other urban and residential developments. At that point in time, Tik Huay's three sons, Yap Peng Heng, Yap Hock Huat, and Yap Kim Choon joined the family business. Converting old pig pens into concrete ponds, they started breeding guppies for local fish exporters.

Also, Ng Yew Kang related the stench to me while we were discussing about various places where he had lived. When he lived at Seletar Hills in the 1970s, there were pig farms in the nearby Seletar Farmways. He actually said, "The pig dung smell pervaded the whole neighbourhood including the Seletar Hills Estate. Because of the air pollution, the Government later decided to phase out pig farming in Singapore. This was because the pig farming industry was heavily pollutive, and also smelled really bad. With respect to the smell, it was especially bad when it rained!"

By the end of 1989, the last of the pig farms, about 200 of them in places like Punggol, Sembawang, Tampines, Changi, and Pulau Ubin, were gone.[30] The Government had announced in April 1985 that it was phasing out pig farms because it was highly pollutive, and used too much land and water. Then-President Leow Leong Poh said at the Livestock Farmers' Association's 16th committee swearing-in ceremony and dinner that he hoped that the authorities would compensate the farmers adequately.

Singapore became independent in 1965 and with independence came rapid economic and social transformation. Aukang was no exception. One significant piece of legislation was the Land Acquisition Act, which overcame the limitations of the Land Acquisition Ordinance of 1955. Although the Ordinance empowered the government to acquire private land compulsorily for public projects, it did not prevent landowners from escalating the prices of their lands, raising the cost of land acquisition and making low-cost public projects challenging or even impossible to develop.

The Land Acquisition Act was approved by Parliament in October 1966 and came into effect in June 1967. It gave the government sweeping powers to acquire vast amounts of private land at below-market rates. As a result, land for public housing, industrial parks, and infrastructure were obtained quickly as the state's decisions could not be challenged in court. As an official statement explained:

> An innovation introduced by the new legislation is that no longer is an appeal by a person aggrieved by an award of the Collector of Land Revenue to lie with the High Court, but to an Appeals Board consisting of a Commissioner of Appeals or a Deputy Commissioner of Appeals, either sitting alone or with two assessors, depending on the quantum of the award appealed against.[31]

Early acquisitions were primarily for public housing built by the HDB and went together with resettlement.

Joseph Tan, who shared his story about his grandfather's home in Aukang and the land they had in Upper Serangoon, also experienced the changes brought about by resettlement. This was his sharing:

> In 1969, while doing my pre-university one [author's note: the first year of pre-university education, or what would be called junior college one or JC one today], I answered the call of my nation and joined the Air Force as a helicopter pilot trainee, putting my formal education on hold. It marked a fulfilling career as a regular RSAF pilot officer in the fledgling and then growing SAF.
>
> In 1972, one year after my return from overseas helicopter training in USA, my family was resettled to a rented HDB flat in Toa Payoh. My grandfather's land had been acquired by HDB for public housing redevelopment...
>
> Although my rented one-roomed HDB flat was smaller than my attap house, it came with tap water, electricity and basic amenities.
>
> Six months later, we bought a 4-room HDB flat in Toa Payoh North for $12,500 under the Government priority resettlement scheme.[32]

There was progress made, which Joseph appreciated, noting the tap water, electricity, and basic amenities, which were not common or easily accessible during the tail end of British colonialism, our days in Malaysia, and the early days of our independence. He also shared how grateful and appreciative he was of the overall progress made by the country over the years:

> As an only son, a brother to six sisters, a father of two, an uncle to many nephews and nieces and a grand uncle to several grandnephews and grandnieces, I have had a relatively good life in the first half of and continuing on, in the second half of my life in Singapore and the world...
>
> Frankly, as always, I am looking forward to a greater and even more gratifying future in Singapore as a Merdeka Generation with and for my family, my extended family, my friends and my fellow Singaporeans.
>
> Thank you for reading.
>
> Majulah Singapura![33]

Many years later, Ngiam Tong Dow reflected on drafting the Cabinet paper setting out the economic and social reasons for the introduction of the Land Acquisition Act:

> ... In principle, the larger interest of the community must take precedence over the rights of the individual. If property rights are absolute, then HDB towns could not have been built to house 85 per cent of our population. The modern city we now call home would have remained a town of slums and swamps.
>
> The core principle of the Land Acquisition Act is that private land can only be acquired for a clear public purpose. In Singapore, private land is compulsorily acquired for infrastructure...
>
> A more difficult problem in land administration is the resettlement of tenants and squatters who do not own the land. The Singapore Government pays what is called ex-gratia compensation. Unlike the landlord, the squatter is not entitled to any legal compensation. The State, out of the goodness of its heart, compensates on the basis of fixed assets, such as his hut and pig-pens. He is offered priority in the allocation [of] flats by the Housing Board, sometimes offered taxi licenses or market stalls, so that he can find alternative means of livelihood.
>
> By being fair to resettled families, public infrastructure has been built for the good of the larger community without public discontent.[54]

While there were some disruptions caused by resettlement, the achievements of the HDB were on the whole remarkable. HDB was a stark improvement over the kampung. My father remarked that he would never want to go back to those times of having no proper housing, sanitation, and electricity.

But he once surprised me by making some remarks regarding noise. He told me that his kampung had a variety of irritating noises throughout the day. The incessant crowing of the cockerel in the morning, the chirping of the crickets in the evening, and the croaking of the toads and frogs after a downpour are now gone.

However, when he left Aukang and moved to his HDB flat in 1975, these noises were soon replaced by new irritants: the pounding of chili in the public flats and the non-stop zooming of motor vehicles along the highways.

Well, I guess it sounds like one cannot avoid noises in a small and crowded country.

Endnotes

1. According to my father, this was most likely attap leaves rather than coconut leaves.
2. Juliana Teo, "I remember Holy Innocents' Lane", in the Singapore Memory Project.
3. Ministry of National Development, "Press Statement: The Control of Rent (Abolition) Bill 2001", Singapore Government Press Release, Ministry of Information and the Arts, 23 February 2002.
4. Joseph Tan's personal account, kindly shared with the author on 11 August 2019.
5. Robert Yeo, *Routes: A Singaporean Memoir 1940–75* (Singapore: Ethos Books, 2014), p. 27.
6. Ibid, pp. 27–28.
7. Juliana Teo, *op cit*.
8. Robert Yeo, *op cit*, p. 28.
9. The Straits Times, "Strikers help pirate service", in *The Straits Times*, 15 November 1955, p. 6.
10. The Straits Times, "The 5-cent pirates", in *The Straits Times*, 29 November 1955, p. 2.
11. This section is based on The Straits Times, "Reward for tip-offs on pirate taxis", in *The Straits Times*, 27 December 1955, p. 5.
12. This section is based on a letter to The Straits Times, "'Private' Taxi", in *The Straits Times*, 5 July 1965, p. 8.
13. The Straits Times, "The pirate taxi strike ends", in *The Straits Times*, 10 March 1966, p. 1.
14. National Heritage Board. "The Singapore Crocodile Farm at Upper Serangoon Road". Source: https://roots.sg/learn/collections/listing/1181586. Updated 2018. Accessed 8 August 2019.
15. Remember Singapore, "The Story of a Crocodile Farm at Upper Serangoon Road". Source: https://remembersingapore.org/2012/07/15/a-crocodile-farm-at-upper-serangoon-road/. Updated 2012. Accessed 8 August 2019.
16. From a chat with Robert Yeo on 1 December 2019.
17. Robert Yeo, *op cit*, p. 76.
18. This account of my grandfather's cinema was actually from my uncle, William Seah. He wrote about it in his personal memoirs and my father and I read about it.
19. You can find out more about mahjong in "History of Gambling in Singapore". Source: https://remembersingapore.org/2011/11/30/4d-mahjong-and-chap-ji-kee/. Updated 2011. Accessed 27 Apr 2019.
20. You can find out more about *see sake* in "History of Gambling in Singapore". Ibid.
21. Paul Tan, "Singing the praises of traditional arts and Teochew opera", in *The Straits Times*, 11 May 2015.
22. Dr Ow Chin Hock, speaking at the NTUC seminar on "The Next Ten Years—Job Creation or Job Loss", at the Singapore Conference Hall, on 10 October 1977.
23. John Kwok, "How Singapore's hawker culture started", in *Today*, 3 April 2019.
24. The Straits Times, "Eggs glut makes farmers sell at a loss", in *The Straits Times*, 23 April 1978, p. 5.

25 This section is based on Teo Lian Huay, "Eggs still sold at the old price", in *New Nation*, 25 January 1979, p. 2.

26 Gerry de Silva, "An urban Punggol tries to preserve part of its past", in *The Straits Times*, 14 June 1988, p. 19.

27 Loh Hui Yin, "We have a role to play, say livestock men", in *Business Times*, 22 March 1984, p. 1.

28 Loh Hui Yin, "Pig farmers meeting soon to discuss their future", in *Business Times*, 14 March 1984, p. 1.

29 History, "Qian Hu Fish Farm Trading". http://www.qianhufish.com/about-us/history. Accessed 27 April 2019.

30 This section is based on The Straits Times, "Last of pig farms to go by end-'89", in *The Straits Times*, 8 March 1988, p. 13.

31 As quoted in The Straits Times, "New Land Acquisition Law Comes into Effect", in *The Straits Times*, 17 June 1967, p. 7.

32 Joseph Tan's personal account, kindly shared with the author on 11 August 2019.

33 Ibid.

34 Ngiam Tong Dow, "Taking Over Private Turf for Public's Good", in *Today*, 2 February 2007, p. 12.

Epilogue

Undeniably, historical Aukang was largely dominated by Teochews, many of whom were Catholics, from the 19th to the 20th century. But in the 21st century, is this still the case today?

Today, while there are still Teochew masses held and prayers chanted at the Church of the Nativity of the Blessed Virgin Mary, and Teochew can occasionally still be heard in the coffee shops, Mandarin and English are widely spoken. Some residents do not even know that the name "Hougang" was once pronounced "Aukang" and instead pronounce the word the "official" Mandarin way. Clearly, the Teochew character and personality of the location has changed over time; change, as people say, is the only constant.

Singaporeans today often refer to the "Kampung Spirit" of the past. They ask questions about it. Was there a real "Kampung Spirit"? If it existed, what was it like?

My personal view is that, while there were challenges living back then, it was also a simpler and more neighbourly time. There was a *gotong royong* spirit of live and let live, a more generous give-and-take spirit. We need to record and reflect upon this so that we can continue this valuable spirit.

This view was shared by others. In 1988, *The Straits Times* reported that Punggol community leaders, including long-time Member of Parliament Ng Kah Ting, were anxious not to lose their special kampung spirit and the *gotong royong* spirit.[1] Punggol as referred to in the article included parts of Aukang, such as Kangkar and the Church of the Nativity. As their kampungs were gradually transformed into suburban public housing estates, local residents were determined to keep the area's special atmosphere and activities that characterised the north-eastern part of Singapore.

Perhaps this kampung spirit existed only in the kampung itself and not in the modern, high-rise HDBs and gleaming condominiums today; perhaps the *gotong royong* spirit was a result of the conditions characteristically present in the kampung itself?

The Yeo family house at 9 Valley Road. Courtesy of Sean Yeo.

Robert Yeo wrote in his memoir about the kampung spirit in Aukang:

> **It was a kampong where the kampong spirit ruled. Among its characteristics was neighbourliness fostered by living in close proximity and by blood relationships. Often these generations lived under one roof and people of the same age groups played together or married one another.[2]**

But I would argue that the kampung itself may be gone, but the kampung spirit can still remain. After all, it really is about neighbourliness and civic-mindedness.

If the kampung spirit is gone, like the physical kampung, we may only have ourselves to blame. Our desire should be to have neighbourly neighbours and be neighbourly neighbours ourselves. Even with modern and high-rise living, we should still retain that *gotong royong* spirit and take special care to be more neighbourly.

Naturally, there were positive views of the vast improvements made. The rapid economic transformation and development of Singapore after independence in 1965 caused the material standard of living to rise dramatically, not just in Hougang, Sengkang, Buangkok, and Punggol, but all around the country.

Epilogue

There were many—naturally not all—who looked forward to and warmly welcomed the progress made, like Joseph Tan. Not everyone was metaphorically taken kicking and screaming from the kampung.

Today, many conveniences and creature comforts are often taken for granted. No one would realistically want to go back to the time of the *tar sai nang*; or go without light when one's father came home late, because he was the only one who knew how to operate the lamp; or scrape together a pitiful living, like many in Singapore did after the War.

Material progress was often rightly celebrated and few would argue that they should go back to the past. And even if we wanted to go back to the past, we cannot. It is unrealistic.

But there were also regrets, and a nostalgic yearning for things lost. And the economic and social developments came at a rapid clip, often unsettling many, who sometimes pined for what was lost. For example: the decline of our own unique localised Teochew dialect; the loss—genuine or perceived—of the kampung spirit; and the disappearance of many historical and physical landmarks... all these were mourned.

In economic terms, not everyone benefited equally from the rapid changes. Landowners who depended on the rental of their lands, or fishermen who depended on the fish from the seas and rivers, or farmers who depended on the produce from the earth were more negatively impacted than those who did not depend on these means of livelihood.

Whatever the perception was of the gains or losses, it is my hope that through this honest and comprehensive account, the history and heritage of the area can and will be remembered. Hopefully, what was of value, like the kampung spirit, the resilience and ruggedness of our people, and the diversity and multi-culturalism amidst a Teochew enclave, can be preserved and remembered.

And a few reflections about identity came to my mind, as I reflected on how the localised Teochew in Aukang (and elsewhere in Singapore too) incorporated words from other languages like Malay. I also reflected on how some Teochew and Catholic practices fused together. As many of the Teochews in Aukang came to work, live, and eventually settle down in the area, they developed a unique sense of who they were.

Is identity primordial, static and fixed, forever unchanging?

My experiences and explorations suggest otherwise. Identity is not set in stone, but evolves gradually over time.

Is a sense of identity then more likely to be developed or nurtured over time, created by our own unique routines, rhythms, and rhymes?

A broader reflection is that there is a larger Singapore Chinese culture and identity, different from a China Chinese culture and identity. While no doubt there are some commonalities between Singapore Chinese and China Chinese, we do have our own unique, separate, and different identity.

From the many personal accounts in this book, we can see clearly that we have our own unique story, dialect, and culture. We are the unique products of our own history.

An evolving Singapore Chinese—or is it more accurately Chinese Singaporean?—identity is what makes us not only Chinese, but Singaporeans. It has multiracial, multicultural, and multireligious elements that have organically come about from more than a century of living in an area with people of different races and cultures, where you can get Hainanese and Babas living harmoniously in a predominantly Teochew population, and where Malays, Indians, and Eurasians could speak Teochew.

And it is this local Chinese culture and identity, and by extension, the larger Singapore identity which we must aim to protect, preserve, and promote.

According to *Channel NewsAsia*, PM Lee Hsien Loong spoke in Mandarin at the *Lianhe Zaobao*'s 95th anniversary gala dinner:

> "Over the years, we have developed our own variation of Chinese culture, and an identity that resonates with the Chinese Singaporeans, as well as with our fellow Singaporeans of other races," Mr Lee said.
>
> "Whatever our race, we are Singaporeans. We are proud of our traditions but we are also committed to building a dynamic future here in Singapore with our fellow Singaporeans."
>
> Mr Lee also said that the promotion of the Chinese culture is an important responsibility and that he hopes all Chinese groups, including Zaobao, will work together to create exciting programmes to encourage others to join them in preserving and promoting Singapore's Chinese culture.
>
> "This will help strengthen our national identity and also inspire the younger generation to deepen their understanding of their own culture and pass it on for generations to come," he said.[3]

And from this whole experience of learning more about the history of my father's kampung and his life there, I have learnt that my father is, all at once, and without contradiction, an Aukang-nang; a Catholic; a Teochew; and a Singaporean.

I will always appreciate going on this journey to better understand where my father came from, what drives him, and who he is.

And by doing so, I have a better understanding of who I am.

Endnotes

1. This paragraph is based on Gerry de Silva, "An urban Punggol tries to preserve part of its past", in *The Straits Times*, 14 June 1988, p. 19.

2. Robert Yeo, *Routes: A Singaporean Memoir 1940–75* (Singapore: Ethos Books, 2014), p. 22.

3. Channel NewsAsia, "Singapore Chinese culture is 'multifaceted and constantly evolving': PM Lee", 6 September 2018.

Bibliography

Bhalla, Shobha Tsering. 2002. "Paradise preserved", in *Today*, 18 April 2002: 37.

Chan Yun Yee, Michelle. 2018. "Punggol: Waves of Recreation", in *MuseSG*, 11, 1.

Channel NewsAsia. 2018. "Singapore Chinese culture is 'multifaceted and constantly evolving': PM Lee", in *Channel NewsAsia*, 6 September 2018.

Channel NewsAsia. 2019. "HDB to launch BTO projects in Punggol inspired by early zoo, fishing village", in *Channel NewsAsia*, 1 September 2019.

Cheow Sue-Ann. 2017. "Sultan's gift holds significance for church", in *The Straits Times*, 19 October 2017.

CHIJ Our Lady of the Nativity. 2017. "School History". Source: https://chijourladyofthenativity.moe.edu.sg/school-information/about-us/school-history. Updated 2017. Accessed 9 September 2019.

Chong, Gillian Pow. 1985. "A feast before the farewell", in *The Straits Times*, 12 November 1985: 13.

Chong Wing Hong. 1985. "Taste of life during the Japanese Occupation", in *The Straits Times*, 28 March 1985: 1.

Choo Woon Hock. 2018. "Koh Yang Kee: From truck driver to logistics leader", in *The Story of Singapore Teochews*. Singapore: Teochew Poit Ip Huay Kuan.

Chow Yaw Huah and Valerie Chew. 2016. "Tou Mu Kung Temple". Source: http://eresources.nlb.gov.sg/infopedia/articles/SIP_1858_2011-12-02.html. Updated 2016. Accessed 23 July 2019.

Chua Seng Chew. 1964. *Report on the Census of Population 1957*. Singapore: Lim Bian Han, Government Printer, Singapore.

Chui Huay Lim Club. 2013. "Introduction". Source: http://www.chuihuaylimclub.com/introduction.html. Updated 2013. Accessed 10 April 2019.

Church of Christ the King. 2003. *Golden Jubilee: Church of the Immaculate Heart of Mary 1953-2003*. Singapore: Church of Christ the King.

Church of the Nativity of the Blessed Virgin Mary. 2016. "History of the Church". Source: http://www.nativity.sg/index.php/history. Updated 2016. Accessed 2 May 2019.

Clammer, John. 1991. *The Sociology of Singapore Religion: Studies in Christianity and Chinese Culture*. Singapore: Chopmen Publishers.

Dabbs, Donald Matheson. 1992. *The History of Gan Eng Seng School*. Singapore: DM Dabbs.

Bibliography

Da Qiao Primary School. 2016. "The Da Qiao Story". Source: http://www.daqiaopri.moe.edu.sg/about-us/the-da-qiao-story. Accessed 13 August 2018.

Del Tufo, M. V. 1949. *Malaya, comprising the Federation of Malaya and the Colony of Singapore: A report on the 1947 census of population*. London: Crown Agents for the Governments of Malaya and Singapore.

Department of Statistics Singapore. 2011. *Singapore Census of Population 2010 Statistical Release 1: Demographic Characteristics, Education, Language and Religion*. Singapore: Department of Statistics.

De Silva, Gerry. 1988. "An urban Punggol tries to preserve part of its past", in *The Straits Times*, 14 June 1988: 19.

Elections Department Singapore. No date. "Parliamentary General Election Results". Retrieved from: https://www.eld.gov.sg/elections_past_parliamentary.html. Accessed 9 December 2019.

Fong, K. K. 1977. "The End of 'Kangkar' Village?", in *New Nation*, 28 April 1977: 2.

Fong, Tanya. 2004. "Temple in legal tussle to be torn down", in *The Straits Times*, 19 August 2004: 7.

Goody Feed Team. 2019. "The story behind the haunted Matilda House in Punggol". Source: https://goodyfeed.com/the-story-behind-the-haunted-matilda-house-in-punggol/. Updated 2019. Accessed 17 July 2019.

Goh, Bryan. 2017. "The Rhythms of a Catholic-Teochew Community: Church, Family and School in Hougang (1945–1981)", for the Department of History, National University of Singapore, AY2016– 2017. 11.

Goh, Bryan. 2018. "The Catholic-Teochew Rhythm: Communal Identity in Hougang, 1945–1981", in *Sojourn: Journal of Social Issues in Southeast Asia*, 33, 1 (March 2018): 227–264.

Goh, Bryan. 2018. "Hougang: Diversity in a Teochew Enclave", in *Muse SG*, 38, 11, Issue 02: 4–11.

Goh Chok Tong. 1996. National Day Rally Speech.

Heng, Michelle. 2017. "Ties that Bind: The Story of Two Brother Poets", in *Biblioasia*, 8 January 2017.

Housing & Development Board. 1981. "HDB Exhumation of Graves", in *The Straits Times*, 17 July 1981: 31.

Housing & Development Board. 2017. "Hougang". Source: http://www.hdb.gov.sg/cs/infoweb/about-us/history/hdb-towns-your-home/hougang. Updated 4 October 2017. Accessed 15 August 2019.

T. F. Hwang. 1989. "T. F. Hwang takes you down Memory Lane", in *The Straits Times*, 29 April 1989: 26.

Johnson, Ian. 2017. "In Singapore, Chinese Dialects Revive After Decades of Restrictions", in *The New York Times*, 26 August 2017.

Koh, Agatha. 1984. "In a Little Parish Church", in *The Straits Times*, 9 December 1984.

Kwok, John. 2019. "How Singapore's hawker culture started", in *Today*, 3 April 2019.

Lee, Edmond. 2000. "Profile of the Singapore Chinese Dialect Groups", in *Statistics Singapore Newsletter*. Singapore: Department of Statistics.

Lee Geok Boi. 1988. "Breakfast in Indian and Teochew Style", in *The Straits Times*, 3 March 1988: 3.

Lee Hsien Loong. 2016. Speech at Montfort School's Centennial Fundraising Dinner on 9 April 2016. Singapore: Prime Minister's Office.

Lee, Joshua. 2019. "Bukit Timah Food Centre was known as '7th Mile'. This is what a 'milestone' really means.", in *Mothership.SG*. Retrieved from: https://mothership.sg/2019/08/bukit-timah-food-centre-milestone/. Accessed 30 August 2019.

Leong Ching. 2018. "Chua Kee Teang: Possibilities in Thorny Problems", in *The Story of Singapore Teochews*. Singapore: Teochew Poit Ip Huay Kuan.

Leong, MT. 1947. "Kew Ong Tai Tay", in *The Singapore Free Press*, 22 October 1947: 4.

Leow, Annabeth. 2017. "School mergers 2019: Merry-go-round of mergers for some affected primary schools", in *The Straits Times*, 20 April 2017.

Lim. 2001. "Temple land case back in court again" in *The Straits Times*, 2 November 2001.

Lim, Cyprian. 2019. *My Maternal Roots: A Story of Family, Faith and Freedom*. Singapore: World Scientific.

Lim, Gillian. 2017. "Church of the Nativity of the Blessed Virgin Mary", in Singapore Infopedia (National Library Board). Source: http://eresources.nlb.gov.sg/infopedia/articles/SIP_1702_2010-09-16.html. Accessed 6 July 2019.

Lim Keng Hoe, James (Accession Number 001935, recorded on 12 August 1997). Oral History Centre, National Archives of Singapore.

Lim Seng (Accession Number 000089; recorded on 28 December 1983). Oral History Centre, National Archives of Singapore.

Lim Yi Han. 2012. "Matilda House gets new life as condo clubhouse", in *The Straits Times*, 18 October 2012.

Loh Hui Yin. 1984. "Pig farmers meeting soon to discuss their future", in *Business Times*, 14 March 1984: 1.

Loh Hui Yin. 1984. "We have a role to play, say livestock men", in *Business Times*, 22 March 1984: 1.

Loh Tuan Lee. 1989. "Matilda House and memories", in *New Paper*, 28 August 1989: 4.

Lone Voice. 1958. "No furniture, club idle", in *The Straits Times*, 22 March 1958: 10.

Low, Augustine. 1986. "Kangkar, once noted for fresh fish and Teochews", in *The Straits Times*, 30 September 1986: 16.

M., G. K. 1929. "The Teochew Cemetery", in *Malaya Tribune*, 11 December 1929: 11.

Majlis Ugama Islam Singapura (MUIS). 2019. Haji Yusoff. Source: https://www.muis.gov.sg/mosque/Our-Mosques/Mosque-Directory/Haji-Yusoff. Accessed 9 August 2019.

Malaya Tribune. 1928. "Refugees from Swatow", in *Malaya Tribune*, 27 March 1928: 7.

Malaya Tribune. 1934. "Municipal Action", in *Malaya Tribune*, 17 May 1934: 7.

Malaya Tribune. 1934. "Local Teachers' Association", in *Malaya Tribune*, 9 July 1934: 18.

Malaya Tribune. 1939. "Overcrowding In A School", in *Malaya Tribune*, 22 June 1939: 7.

Malaya Tribune. 1949. "Asst. Director of Education", in *Malaya Tribune*, 18 February 1949: 2.

Ministry of National Development. 2001. "Press Statement: The Control of Rent (Abolition) Bill 2001". Singapore Government Press Release, Ministry of Information and the Arts, 23 February 2002.

Montfort School. 1990. "In loving memory: Madam Maria Lee Kin (1901–1990)", in *Montfort Annual 1990*, Singapore.

Nanda, Akshita. 2015. "Work of lost Malayan poet Teo Poh Leng republished after 78 years thanks to ST article", in *The Straits Times*, 12 October 2015.

Nanda, Akshita. 2018. "Teater Ekamatra's Tiger of Malaya presents perils of oversimplifying history", in *The Straits Times*, 20 September 2018.

National Heritage Board. 2018. "The Singapore Crocodile Farm at Upper Serangoon Road". Source: https://roots.sg/learn/collections/listing/1181586. Accessed 8 August 2019.

National Heritage Board. 2016. "Tou Mu Kung Temple". Source: https://roots.sg/Content/Places/national-monuments/tou-mu-kung-temple. Accessed 23 July 2019.

New Nation. 1981. "Exhumation", in *New Nation*, 21 July 1981: 2.

Ng, Daniel. 2015. "Matilda House". Source: https://stateofbuildings.sg/places/matilda-house. Updated 2015. Accessed 17 July 2019.

Ng Mia Yong. 1929. "The Teochew Cemetery", in *Malaya Tribune*, 16 December 1929: 5.

Ng, Serene. 2013. Interview with Mdm Chong Ah Yong, in Singapore Memory Project.

Ngiam Tong Dow. 2007. "Taking Over Private Turf for Public's Good", in *Today*, 2 February 2007.

Ogihara-Schuck, Eriko. 2016. "Teo Kah Leng's Malayan Poetry", in Teo Kah Leng, *I Found A Bone and Other Poems*. Singapore: Ethos Books.

Ow Chin Hock. 1977. Speech at the "The Next Ten Years—Job Creation or Job Loss", at the Singapore Conference Hall, 10 October 1977.

Pang Cheng Lian. 1971. "Lee pays respect to PAP stalwart", in *New Nation*, 29 June 1971: 2.

Perera, Audrey. 1986. "Kangkar village draws fond ex-residents back", in *The Straits Times*, 21 December 1986: 22.

Phillips, Percival. 1930. "Sir Percival Phillips goes to Punggol", in *The Singapore Free Press and Mercantile Advertiser*, 14 January 1930: 18.

Punggol Community Club. 1993. *Punggol Community Club (Official Opening) Souvenir Magazine*, 13 March 1993, Singapore.

Qian Hu Corporation. History, "Qian Hu Fish Farm Trading". Source: http://www.qianhufish.com/about-us/history. Accessed 27 April 2019.

Raymond, Jose. 2002. "Mystery behind the last 'palace' standing in Punggol", in *Today*, 3 September 2002: 1.

Remember Singapore. 2010. "Punggol Matilda House". Source: https://remembersingapore.org/punggol-matilda-house/. Accessed 17 July 2019.

Remember Singapore. 2011. 4D, Mahjong and Chap Ji Kee. History of Gambling in Singapore. Source: https://remembersingapore.org/2011/11/30/4d-mahjong-and-chap-ji-kee/. Accessed 27 Apr 2019.

Remember Singapore. 2012. "The Story of a Crocodile Farm at Upper Serangoon Road". Source: https://remembersingapore.org/2012/07/15/a-crocodile-farm-at-upper-serangoon-road/. Accessed 8 August 2019.

Remember Singapore. 2014. Searching for Singapore's Last Water Wells.

Source: https://remembersingapore.org/2014/04/19/singapores-last-water-wells/. Accessed 4 August 2019.

Roman Catholic Archdiocese of Singapore. 2019. "Parish Information: Church of the Immaculate Heart of Mary". Source: https://www.catholic.sg/directory/singapore_catholic_church/church-parish-information/?Ox45Q=29. Accessed 29 January 2019.

Roman Catholic Archdiocese of Singapore. 2019. "The Brothers of St Gabriel (SG)". Source: http://history.catholic.sg/the-brothers-of-st-gabriel-sg/. Accessed 10 April 2019.

Seah, Lynn. 2016. *The Story of Montfort, 1916–2016: Age Quod Agis*, Singapore: Straits Times Press.

Seah, Shawn. 2019. *Leader and Legislator—Seah Liang Seah*. Singapore: Pagesetters.

Seah, Shawn. 2019. *Seah Eu Chin: His Life and Times* (2nd Ed.). Singapore: Pagesetters.

Serangoon Gardens Commemorative Magazine Editorial Committee. 1994. *Serangoon Gardens: 35th anniversary, 1959–1994*, Singapore: Serangoon Gardens Commemorative Magazine Editorial Committee.

Serangoon Secondary School. 2017. "School History". Updated 2017. Source: https://serangoonsec.moe.edu.sg/about-us/school-history. Accessed 3 December 2019.

Serangoon Secondary School. 2017. "SSS Alumni". Updated 2017. Source: https://serangoonsec.moe.edu.sg/partnership/sss-alumni. Accessed 3 December 2019.

Singapore Film Locations Archive. 2012. "Tiger of Malaya (1943)". Source: https://sgfilmlocations.com/2014/08/17/tiger-of-malaya-1943/. Accessed 20 August 2019.

Singapore Government Press Release. 1997. "Speech by DPM Lee Hsien Loong at the launch of National Education on 17 May 97 at TCS TV Theatre at 9.30A.M.", Media Division, Ministry of Information and The Arts.

Singapore Police Force. 2015. *Setia Dan Bakti: 50 Stories of Loyalty and Service*. Singapore: Singapore Police Force.

Singh, Kirpal. 1980. "Meet the Grand Old Man of Singapore Letters...", in *The Straits Times*, 18 May 1980: 1.

St Paul's Church. 2019. "Our History". Source: http://www.st.paulschurch.org.sg/. Updated 2018. Accessed on 31 July 2019.

Sua, Tracy. 2005. "Four new heritage sites", in *The Straits Times*, 14 January 2005: 10.

TAB. 1929. "The Teochew Cemetery", in *Malaya Tribune*, 20 November 1929: 11.

Tan, Cephah. 1989. "Duo unearth Japanese and Qing artifacts at Punggol Beach", in *The Straits Times*, 11 October 1989: 3.

Tan, C. H. 1929. "The Teochew Cemetery", in *Malaya Tribune*, 27 November 1929: 11.

Tan Gia Lim. 2018. *An Introduction to the Culture and History of the Teochews in Singapore*. Singapore: World Scientific.

Tan Kog Enn. 2018. "Ng Hoy Keng: Driving Ambition", in *The Story of Singapore Teochews*. Singapore: Teochew Poit Ip Huay Kuan.

Tan, L. C. 1929. "Teochew Cemetery", in *The Straits Times*, 8 November 1929: 19.

Tan, L. C. 1929. "The Teochew Cemetery", in *Malaya Tribune*, 12 November 1929: 11.

Tan, L. C. 1931. "The Teochew Cemetery", in *Malaya Tribune*, 10 April 1931: 2.

Tan, Paul. 2015. "Singing the praises of traditional arts and Teochew opera", in *The Straits Times*, 11 May 2015.

Tan, Rachel. 2013. "Matilda, a grand old house in Punggol", in *The Sunday Times*, 2 September 2013.

Tay, Frank. (Accession Number 003554; recorded on 23 August 2010). Oral History Centre, National Archives of Singapore.

Teo Cheng Wee. 2014. "Growing Teochew Roots", in *The Straits Times*, 10 November 2014.

Teo, Eisen. 2020. *Jalan Singapura: 700 Years of Movement in Singapore*. Singapore: Marshall Cavendish.

Teo, Juliana. "I remember Holy Innocents' Lane", in the *Singapore Memory Project*.

Teo Kah Leng. 2016. *I Found A Bone and Other Poems*. Singapore: Ethos Books.

Teochew Poit Ip Huay Kuan. 2018. *The Story of Singapore Teochews*. Singapore: Teochew Poit Ip Huay Kuan.

Teo Lian Huay. 1979. "Eggs still sold at the old price", in *New Nation*, 25 January 1979: 2.

The Basapas of Singapore. 2011. "W.L.S. Basapa". Source: http://www.singaporebasapa.com/W.L.S.%20Basapa%20The%20"Animal%20Man".html. Accessed 13 August 2019.

The Helping Hand. 2015. "Our Mission". Source: http://thehelpinghand.org.sg/our-organization/our-mission/. Updated 2015. Accessed on 31 July 2019.

The New Paper. 1989. "War relic turns junkyard", in *The New Paper*, 14 July 1989: 3.

The Singapore Free Press. 1953. "A New Catholic Church", in *The Singapore Free Press*, 12 December 1953: 5.

The Singapore Free Press. 1954. "This is a Happy Suburb", in *The Singapore Free Press*, 31 May 1954: 7.

The Singapore Free Press. 1954. "Boys Are Proud of Their Club", in *The Singapore Free Press*, 25 June 1954: 14.

The Singapore Free Press. 1955. "The Big Vote Trek", in *The Singapore Free Press*, 19 March 1955: 7.

The Singapore Free Press. 1958. "Hard work call to colony's leaders", in *The Singapore Free Press*, 3 June 1958: 1.

The Singapore Free Press and Mercantile Advertiser. 1843. "Untitled", in *The Singapore Free Press and Mercantile Advertiser*, 26 January 1843: 1.

The Singapore Free Press and Mercantile Advertiser. 1851. "Untitled", in *The Singapore Free Press and Mercantile Advertiser*, 5 March 1851: 1.

The Singapore Free Press and Mercantile Advertiser. 1855. "The Free Press", in *The Singapore Free Press and Mercantile Advertiser*, 12 April 1855: 2.

The Singapore Free Press and Mercantile Advertiser. 1856. "Municipal Committee", in *The Singapore Free Press and Mercantile Advertiser*, 13 November 1856: 3.

The Singapore Free Press and Mercantile Advertiser. 1917. "Untitled", in *The Singapore Free Press and Mercantile Advertiser*, 19 May 1917: 7.

The Singapore Free Press and Mercantile Advertiser. 1934. "Funeral Of Mr. Nishimura", in *The Singapore Free Press and Mercantile Advertiser*, 8 December 1934: 6.

The Singapore Free Press and Mercantile Advertiser. 1938. "Headmaster on Malayan Education", in *The Singapore Free Press and Mercantile Advertiser*, 6 July 1938: 7.

The Singapore Free Press and Mercantile Advertiser. 1939. "Untitled", in *The Singapore Free Press and Mercantile Advertiser*, 19 August 1939: 4.

The Straits Times. 1850. "Untitled", in *The Straits Times*, 9 July 1850: 5.

The Straits Times. 1851. "Untitled", in *The Straits Times*, 28 January 1851: 5.

The Straits Times. 1855. "Untitled", in *The Straits Times*, 1 May 1855: 4.

The Straits Times. 1855. "Untitled", in *The Straits Times*, 15 May 1855: 5.

The Straits Times. 1896. "Roman Catholic Chinese", in *The Straits Times*, 22 January 1896: 2.

The Straits Times. 1933. "Appeal to Local Teachers", in *The Straits Times*, 27 February 1933: 6.

Bibliography

The Straits Times. 1946. "Spotlight on Malaya and Malayans", in *The Straits Times*, 22 September 1946: 2.

The Straits Times. 1947. "All-Day Gunfire in 1942 Massacre", in *The Straits Times*, 12 March 1947: 1.

The Straits Times. 1950. "On The Margin", in *The Straits Times*, 5 April 1950: 6.

The Straits Times. 1953. "Upper Serangoon boys' club formed", in *The Straits Times*, 6 January 1953: 7.

The Straits Times. 1953. "New community centre in S'pore", in *The Straits Times*, 21 April 1953: 8.

The Straits Times. 1953. "They used to pray: spare us from tigers", in *The Straits Times*, 2 August 1953: 3.

The Straits Times. 1953. "Church to be blessed", in *The Straits Times*, 13 December 1953: 9.

The Straits Times. 1955. "Strikers help pirate service", in *The Straits Times*, 15 November 1955: 6.

The Straits Times. 1955. "The 5-cent pirates", in *The Straits Times*, 29 November 1955: 2.

The Straits Times. 1955. "Reward for tip-offs on pirate taxis", in *The Straits Times*, 27 December 1955: 5.

The Straits Times. 1956. "The One That Didn't Get Away", in *The Straits Times*, 22 April 1956: 3.

The Straits Times. 1957. "Dramatic club", in *The Straits Times*, 12 August 1957: 7.

The Straits Times. 1959. "Ex-Lib-Soc leader fights 3 newcomers", in *The Straits Times*, 21 May 1959: 5.

The Straits Times. 1965. "'Private' Taxi", in *The Straits Times*, 5 July 1965: 8.

The Straits Times. 1966. "The pirate taxi strike ends", in *The Straits Times*, 10 March 1966: 1.

The Straits Times. 1967. "New Land Acquisition Law Comes into Effect", in *The Straits Times*, 17 June 1967.

The Straits Times. 1973. "Japanese Cemetery Closed to Burials", in *The Straits Times*, 9 May 1973: 21.

The Straits Times. 1977. "Bridge to link two roads", in *The Straits Times*, 29 April 1977: 12.

The Straits Times. 1978. "Eggs glut makes farmers sell at a loss", in *The Straits Times*, 23 April 1978: 5.

The Straits Times. 1979. "CC to shift", in *The Straits Times*, 13 July 1979: 13.

The Straits Times. 1979. "Kangka CC", in *The Straits Times*, 27 August 1979: 8.

The Straits Times. 1983. "Hougang links to expressways", in *The Straits Times*, 16 March 1983: 10.

The Straits Times. 1983. "Farewell Kangkar", in *The Straits Times*, 17 June 1983: 2.

The Straits Times. 1983. "Auctioning will go on at new site", in *The Straits Times*, 17 June 1983: 4.

The Straits Times. 1984. "Closing date", in *The Straits Times*, 3 October 1984: 16.

The Straits Times. 1986. "Graves to be exhumed", in *The Straits Times*, 4 August 1986: 10.

The Straits Times. 1988. "Last of pig farms to go by end-'89", in *The Straits Times*, 8 March 1988: 13.

The Straits Times. 1988. "Fort ruins in Punggol may be turned into tourist attraction", in *The Straits Times*, 14 June 1988: 1.

The Straits Times. 1998. "The well returns to Tua Jia Ka", in *The Straits Times*, 27 October 1998: 31.

Toh Yong Chuan. "BreadTalk founder is new Teochew clan leader", *The Straits Times*, Thursday 4 April 2013.

Urban Redevelopment Authority. 2019. "Matilda House". Source: https://www.ura.gov.sg/Conservation-Portal/Explore/History?bldgid=PGLRD. Accessed 17 July 2019.

Wee, Paul. 1977. "Macabre find at Punggol", in *The Straits Times*, 14 March 1977: 1.

Wijeysingha, Eugene. 2013. *Down the Seletar River: Discovering a Hidden Treasure of Singapore*. Singapore: Seletar Hills Estate Residents' Association.

Wong Kim Hoh. 2012. "GIC Chief's Unlikely Fishing Village Roots", in *The Straits Times*, 8 April 2012, p. 33.

Yeo, George. 2002. Speech at The Teochew Experience: An Exhibition on the Teochew Community in Singapore, 3 October 2002. Media Relations Division, Ministry of Information, Communications and the Arts.

Yeo, Nicholas. 2012. "The Church of the Nativity of the Blessed Virgin Mary: 160 years and counting", in *The Lion Raw*. Source: https://lionraw.com/2012/01/16/385/. Updated 16 January 2012. Accessed 6 July 2019.

Yeo, Robert. 2014. *Routes: A Singaporean Memoir 1940–75*, Singapore: Ethos Books.

Yuen Sin. 2012. "Our Forgotten Zoo", in *The New Paper*, 18 July 2012.

Yuen Sin. 2019. "Teochew v Teochew: From 'twin brothers' to combatants in court", in *The Sunday Times*, 10 March 2019, p. A4.

Zaccheus, Melody. 2019. "Teochew Immigrant's Role in Founding Catholic High", in *The Straits Times*, 22 May 2019.

Acknowledgements

I am grateful to the many people who have contributed to this book. It would not have been possible to complete it without their kind and generous help.

First, I have to thank my family. Thank you, **Daddy**. Without you, this book would have been impossible for me to write. My supportive **Mummy** was a key part of this project. Special thanks must go to **Uncle William** and **Aunty Florence**.

Second, the people who spoke to me or my father, or shared their accounts and experiences with me, deserve special mention. Thank you, **Robert Yeo**, **Lee Tong Juan**, **Lee Boon Kee**, **S. Lim**, **B. Goh**, **Lynn Lim**, **Joseph Tan**, **Ng Yew Kang**, **Foong Tai Wei**, **John Liow**, **Edmund M. Arozoo**, **Marc Sebastian Rerceretnam**, and **Cyprian Lim**. The members of **Montfort Alumni** were kind, generous, and helpful: **Toh Tong Dee**; **Bernard Yeo**; **Nicholas Yeo**; and **Sarafian**.

Photo credits and thanks to **S. Lim**; **Sean Yeo and family**; **Sarafian** and his father, **Encik Salleh Sariman**; and **Edmund M Arozoo** and the late **Harold Arozoo**.

Third, the book would not have been possible without the help and support of **Khoo Yee Hong** and my wonderful editor, **Sylvia Koh**, and the kind people at **World Scientific**.

Fourth, I have to thank my mentors and teachers in my writing journey. I am especially grateful to **Robert Yeo** for his kindness, guidance, and direction; **Dr John Kwok**, who encouraged not only my first and second books, but also my third, providing valuable input.

Fifth, I also appreciate those who gave me leads and pointers. A unique acknowledgement must go to **Leow Xian Zu**; one lead he gave me was of his grandfather, businessman and association leader Leow Leong Poh. Special thanks must go to **Kelvin Ang** for his support, and **Victor Yue** for his encouragement and help. I want to thank **Khoo Ee Hoon** for giving me guidance and pointers on an early draft. And thanks to **TGL** for correcting my mathematics so that I could be accurate. I appreciate everything they have done for the cause of heritage in Singapore.

Sixth, I would like to thank the **Singapore Seah Clan Association** for their generous support. Special thanks must go to **Jeremy Seah Han Chong**.

Last, but certainly not least, I worked with an amazing team of volunteers and project managers. **Claudia's** kindness and support have been invaluable; she took care of administration, marketing, and finances. Special thanks must also go to **Goh Siak Wei** for his assistance, research, and support. **Wilson Yeo** helped me in administration. **Jeyasoorya's** artwork was amazing; I am truly grateful for her. Also, special thanks to the dedicated, hardworking volunteers of **Record & Reflect**: **Reuben Ng, Goh Siak Zhiang,** and **Dingfeng**. I benefited from **Tilve Tarini Sachin**, whose research assistance and writing skills contributed to this book.

The works cited in this book are documented in the bibliography. Materials used in my reconstruction of this narrative are within the bounds of fair usage.

However, should you find any incorrectly attributed or inaccurate material, please inform me so that I can make the appropriate changes in future. My experience has taught me that you can check, double check, triple check, and have proof-readers, editors, experts, friends, and family checking your work, and there will still be mistakes.

However, one has to take personal responsibility. All mistakes and omissions are mine, and I apologise for them.

About the Author

Shawn Seah is the author of *Seah Eu Chin: His Life & Times* (1st edition 2017, 2nd edition 2019) and *Leader and Legislator– Seah Liang Seah* (2019), and a public speaker on local history and heritage. He has been part of the Singapore Heritage Festival, and has given many talks and lectures in venues such as the Peranakan Museum; Fort Canning Centre during the Singapore Bicentennial; and even a Chinese Confucian temple, the Nanyang Sacred Union.

Shawn holds a Master's degree in Economic History (Distinction) from the London School of Economics and Political Science, and a Bachelor's degree in Economics (First Class Honours), with a minor in History, from the National University of Singapore. He also holds a Postgraduate Diploma in Education (Distinction) from the National Institute of Education. He is interested in Singapore's history and heritage, as well as economic development in Southeast Asia.

With work experience in education, policy development, and communications and engagement, Shawn's aim as an author is to make history appealing and relevant.

About the Artist

Jeyasoorya is a Singapore-based illustrator who earned her Bachelor's degree in Fine Arts with honours from Lasalle College of the Arts. She is currently creating paintings geared towards children and enjoys working on whimsical, narrative-driven pieces.

www.ingramcontent.com/pod-product-compliance
Lightning Source LLC
Chambersburg PA
CBHW052057230426
43662CB00037B/1985